IMPOSTER SYNDROME ANECDOTES

Techniques for Overcoming Imposter Syndrome
and Live the Life of Your Dreams

Tony Bennis

TABLE OF CONTENTS

PART THREE: BODY LANGUAGE AND CONFIDENCE

PART FOUR: EXERCISES FOR
OVERCOMING IMPOSTER SYNDROME

INTRODUCTION

Although it's not an official health condition, imposter syndrome is an experience many have. As well, it can lead to or be associated with feelings of anxiety, depression, stress, and other mental health conditions.

If you picked up this book, chances are you've had your own run in with imposter syndrome. You might recognize it as being a sensation of being a fraud, an imposter, or as if you have somehow 'tricked' people into believing you are something you are not. This feeling can be uncomfortable, overwhelming, and self-sabotaging. Especially if you are not clear as to what it is or where it comes from.

The reality is: imposter syndrome can strike anyone. Further, it doesn't necessarily mean you are incapable, tricking anyone, or that you were chosen by mistake. Instead, it has more to do with how you view yourself, the expectations you've placed on yourself, and how you feel in relation to the people around you or the attention you are receiving from them.

In *Imposter Syndrome Anecdotes: Techniques for Overcoming Imposter Syndrome And Live The Life Of Your Dreams* we are going to explore this phenomenon at a deeper level. Together, we will uncover what it is, where it comes from, why it strikes, and how it impacts people. We will also explore different techniques you can use to overcome imposter syndrome and feel confident and secure in your life and achievements.

Whether this is a new experience for you, or it is one that you have struggled with frequently throughout your life, there is a way to overcome it and recover from the jarring symptoms it creates. By the time you have finished this book you will have all the tools you need to overcome it *for good.*

There is one caveat, however. Many people come under the belief that if they know better, they'll do better. Have you heard this saying before? Perhaps it's true in some scenarios, but I've discovered that this is not always the case. When it comes to matters concerning your mind and the thoughts and emotions you are experiencing, knowing better is not always the answer.

Knowledge is only power when it is *applied.* That means that in addition to reading this book you <u>must</u> also commit to applying the techniques we discuss *consistently* in order to see real change in your imposter syndrome.

The more you repeat these tools in different scenarios that trigger imposter syndrome for you, the stronger they become.

Thus, the more effective they are at defeating imposter syndrome and creating a sensation of calm, peace, and confidence.

If you are ready to learn how *and* apply the techniques you learn consistently until you get your desired results, it's time to get started! Let's dig in with a deep dive into what imposter syndrome *really* is!

PART ONE

WHAT IS IMPOSTER SYNDROME?

CHAPTER 1

What Is Imposter Syndrome?

"We can't all be imposters, can we?"
– Dr. Jessamy Hibberd

Imposter syndrome is a phenomenon that creates a disturbing mental experience for people who have it. While it is not an official medical condition or mental health concern, it is attached to real feelings that can be overwhelming and sometimes even unbearable for people experiencing it.

What Are the Symptoms?

This phenomenon has been said to be more likely to arise in perfectionists or high achievers. Women are more likely to experience it than men. When it strikes, the person experiencing it generally feels a sense of self-doubt that can be either mild or incredibly crippling.

That self-doubt can create thoughts like:

- "They have mischaracterized me; I do not deserve this."
- "They think I'm better than I am, I'm going to ruin this."
- "What if I'm not capable of meeting their expectations?"
- "What if I go to do this and I forget everything, and they think I'm a fraud?"
- "What if they made a mistake picking me? Someone else would have been better."
- "My results were based on luck; I don't deserve this, and I can't replicate it."

This mental chatter can be distressing, particularly if you are attached to the experience that is triggering it. For example, if you recently took on new responsibilities in your career you might be feeling imposter syndrome. While you likely have the exact skills to thrive with these new responsibilities it might *feel* like you don't, and your self-doubt begins to convince you that there's been a mistake.

Another common symptom of imposter syndrome is called the "Imposter Cycle." In this cycle, you frantically plan and do everything you can to avoid making any mistakes, or you procrastinate and then do frantic last-minute planning and preparation for the event which is triggering imposter syndrome. Then, when it's over and you feel great, you experience a rush of excitement and relief. When another event arises that triggers your imposter syndrome the cycle begins again.

Why Do People Experience Imposter Syndrome?

All of these symptoms of imposter syndrome are believed to be caused by the individual having exceedingly high expectations of themselves combined with a strong fear of failing or letting anyone down. Not surprisingly, people who deal with imposter syndrome frequently report coming from a family who valued success and punished or frowned upon failure. Not all individuals come from this background, however, yet many individuals claim to have a similar feeling of pressure and overwhelm stemming from society.

In many individuals, imposter syndrome is experienced because they feel that if they could do things perfectly, or near perfectly, they would be liked more. They might think this is where the ultimate praise and validation comes from and believe that unless they can reach that they are not worthy or valuable.

This unfortunate belief can create anxiety, depression, and imposter syndrome in the individual struggling with it. It can also lead to people trying exceedingly hard to live up to astronomical expectations and always feeling like "real success" is just beyond where they can reach. This cycle becomes exhausting and is entirely unsustainable. Breaking free from it and creating more realistic expectations for yourself is essential if you want to recover from it.

What Does Imposter Syndrome Affect?

If you struggle with imposter syndrome, chances are you experience it in many areas of your life. While it may be most prominent in one area, such as your profession or academics, if you were to look at your entire life, you'd likely notice it in other areas, too.

Here is a list of examples of how imposter syndrome can affect the different areas of your life. Read through each list and notice which ones stand out to you. You will want to apply the techniques in this book to each area of your life being affected so you can completely recover from this painful and sabotaging belief set.

Professionally

Imposter syndrome can negatively impact your professional life by causing you to believe that your success is the result of luck rather than skill. This can lead to you to feel like Alicia who was recently promoted to partner at her law firm. The thought of trying to prove herself worthy of the title lead to her over-investing in different projects to ensure nothing went wrong. Despite being completely worthy of the promotion and capable of the work it entails she began to underestimate the value she brought to her firm. The experience left her crippled with anxiety and seeking support to overcome what she quickly identified as being a case of imposter syndrome. Fortunately, she recognized it well before it developed into burnout because she had experienced the same symptoms of imposter syndrome years earlier when she was studying in law school.

Academically

Although Alicia experienced it in school, I know of someone else who also experienced a phenomenal case of imposter syndrome when he was attending university. Chris was attending university to become an investment banker when he realized he was feeling out of his league. In an attempt to follow in his father and grandfather's footsteps he aimed to become the top of his class. Whenever he received a lower grade, he would experience severe anxiety that made studying feel even more all-consuming. Within two years he was completely burnt out and struggling to keep up with any expectations. He began failing classes, refused to go home to visit his family for the holidays, and start to drink a little too much to make up for the shame he felt. Fortunately, he was able to have a serious chat with his dad and felt some relief from his imposter syndrome. By the end of his third year his grades were up again, and he finished with excellent grades and a much higher sense of self-esteem and self-confidence.

In Relationships

In relationships imposter syndrome can lead to individuals feeling unprepared, unworthy, and doubtful. Ryan was a newlywed when he began experiencing imposter syndrome. For him, it felt like a fear that his new wife would realize he wasn't that great of a guy and would ultimately leave him. When they had their first baby the imposter syndrome became so bad that Ryan began looking for reasons to leave. Finally, his wife confronted him on his behavior. She said he had been doing too much and that, whenever she tried to connect with him, he would become closed off. Ryan admitted that he was trying to make up for being a poor husband and father and that he was afraid of her realizing this and leaving him. When she explained that she did not feel that way and all and had no intention of leaving he realized he had a case of imposter syndrome and needed to seek help to move past it.

In Your Self-Image

Lastly, imposter syndrome can have a negative impact on your self-image. When you frequently succumb to the negative symptoms of your imposter syndrome you are more likely to get trapped in cycles where you feel worthless, hopeless, and helpless. It might start out small or hardly noticeable at first, but over time it becomes substantial and can create a serious issue with your self-image. A poor self-image can lead to low self-esteem and low self-confidence which results in you inserting yourself into low quality or toxic circumstances professionally, academically, and socially. Recovering from imposter syndrome can help you change the narrative of your life and enjoy a healthier self-image and healthier relationships, studies, and professions as a result.

Chapter Summary

Imposter syndrome is not an official mental health diagnosis, but it is an incredibly challenging phenomenon to experience all the same. Many people attend therapy each year to discover they have imposter syndrome and learn ways of coping with or recovering from it. I'll show you those ways in this book.

So far, you know:

- What imposter syndrome is
- What the symptoms are
- Why it affects people
- Who it affects
- How it affects them

By now you have likely identified imposter syndrome in yourself and are ready to take the necessary steps to overcome it – for good.

CHAPTER 2

Tools and Methods for Combatting Imposter Syndrome

"Nothing can harm you as much as your own thoughts unguarded." – Buddha

Throughout this book we will discuss many tools that assist you with overcoming imposter syndrome. These tools will create a means for you to not only silence but eliminate the self-doubt that fuels imposter syndrome so you can enjoy a higher quality of life.

Before we dive into them, I want to review them so you understand what each tool is used for, why it is essential, and how it will help. While this book was written in order of how you ideally should address your imposter syndrome with helpful psychological, physical, and lifestyle tools, this doesn't mean you *must* use these tools in order. Often, a helpful way to approach life change is to start with what feels accessible for you and use that to fuel momentum for change.

Psychological Tools for Imposter Syndrome

Since imposter syndrome is fueled by a serious case of self-doubt psychological tools are a logical and useful response to combatting this syndrome. The psychological tools that aid in overcoming imposter syndrome are designed to help you re-wire your brain to heal and eliminate the crippling self-doubt that leads to imposter syndrome in the first place.

Similar to exercising with weights to build muscle, psychological tools need to be used repetitively to reinforce their strength. The value of a psychological tool is that it quite literally *rewires* your brain by creating neural pathways that are different from the ones that have been fueling your self-doubt. Neural pathways are developed through repetition which is why you want to consistently apply these skills until you see meaningful results.

Physical Tools for Imposter Syndrome

Our bodies are operating with a system called "biofeedback." Biofeedback means that what happens in my body affects what is going on in my mind. An example of biofeedback is when something scares you and it causes your heart to begin racing. Almost instantaneously your adrenaline and cortisol levels spike and your thoughts closely follow with ones that reflect stress, anxiety, and fear.

Similar to how biofeedback can trigger overwhelming reactions it can also be used to heal unwanted ones. With imposter syndrome biofeedback can be used to stimulate feelings of self-confidence and self-esteem. The result is that you begin to think and feel in accordance with how you are carrying yourself. This can best be described as a real-world and effective version of "fake it 'til you make it."

Exercises That Defeat Imposter Syndrome

In addition to psychological and physical tools that can defeat imposter syndrome there are also exercises that can assist you by adjusting your mindset, beliefs, and lifestyle to overcome imposter syndrome. I have grouped these into their own category because they are not intended to be done as repetitively as the psychological and physical tools are. Instead, they are intended to facilitate profound breakthrough moments that allow you to see things differently and alter your way of thinking and living relatively quickly.

You may want to skip ahead to this section if you are struggling particularly badly, but I caution you against *staying* in it. The primary reason is that it can be easy to create a breakthrough experience, feel like you are 'all healed,' and then stop doing the work. As a result, your symptoms come back relatively quickly, and it can become a negative cycle of suffering and relief. Instead, if you skip ahead and create a breakthrough, ensure you then come back to the psychological and physical tools and maintain the results that breakthrough created. This way, you experience lasting relief from imposter syndrome.

The Essential Key: Consistency

The final tool which I will reference throughout this book, yet does not have its own section, is *consistency*. As I mentioned in the introduction, a lack of consistency leads to you not internalizing and assimilating the results that can be created with this book.

It is essential that you do not just *do* the work, but you *become the result* of the work. This is where you change yourself on an identity-level and imposter syndrome *no longer has anywhere to take root in your life. As a result, you are fully recovered.*

This outcome is preferential to spending your life trying to cope with distressing and disturbing symptoms, as it means you no longer have a reason to experience them in the first place. This is the result I aspire to create with you in *Imposter Syndrome Anecdotes.*

Chapter Summary

There are many tools that can assist you with overcoming imposter syndrome. The best combat for this phenomenon is a series of tools that affect your mental, emotional, and physical wellbeing. The tools we cover in this book are:

- Psychological tools that work on your mindset and beliefs
- Physical tools that work through a process called biofeedback

- Exercises that can help facilitate mental and emotional breakthroughs
- Consistency which is the tool that makes all the other tools work

If you are ready to implement these tools and are committed to remaining consistent until you see the results you want, the rest of the book awaits!

CHAPTER 3

Imposter Syndrome Test

*"Acknowledge your fear, understand it, and then
get comfortable existing in a space with it."*
– Allie Dattilio

This chapter is intended to help you better understand what symptoms you might be experiencing in your journey with imposter syndrome. It is *not* a diagnosis for mental health conditions or *any* condition. By taking this test you will have a deeper awareness of how much you might be struggling with these feelings and how they are affecting your life. It is intended only to help you develop a greater sense of self-awareness so you can take a more holistic approach to recovering from the troubling thoughts and emotions that imposter syndrome can create.

The Quiz Rules

Pick the answers that are most appropriate to your experience with each question. It is a good idea to write these down, so you don't forget. When we're done, we'll discuss what your answers mean.

The Quiz

1. Regardless of how much I fear doing poorly on a test or task, I generally do well.

    a. Never

    b. Rarely

    c. Sometimes

    d. Often

    e. Always

2. Others believe I am more capable than I truly am.

    a. Never

    b. Rarely

    c. Sometimes

    d. Often

    e. Always

3. I avoid being evaluated by others and dread others' evaluations of me.

  a. Never
  b. Rarely
  c. Sometimes
  d. Often
  e. Always

4. I am afraid I won't live up to people's expectations of me, especially when they have praised me for a previous accomplishment.

  a. Never
  b. Rarely
  c. Sometimes
  d. Often
  e. Always

5. I tend to attribute my past or current success to luck, right timing, or knowing the right people.

  a. Never
  b. Rarely
  c. Sometimes
  d. Often
  e. Always

6. I am terrified that someone will expose me as being incapable or unqualified, especially to the point I deem important in my life.

  a. Never
  b. Rarely
  c. Sometimes
  d. Often
  e. Always

7. My memories are more focused on times when I didn't do my best, rather than times when I did.

  a. Never
  b. Rarely
  c. Sometimes
  d. Often
  e. Always

8. I rarely perform as well as I'd hoped on a task or project I take on.

  a. Never
  b. Rarely
  c. Sometimes
  d. Often
  e. Always

9. My success is sometimes the result of an error.

    a. Never

    b. Rarely

    c. Sometimes

    d. Often

    e. Always

10. I have a hard time accepting praise or compliments from others about my accomplishments or intelligence.

    a. Never

    b. Rarely

    c. Sometimes

    d. Often

    e. Always

11. My success is often the result of luck.

    a. Never

    b. Rarely

    c. Sometimes

    d. Often

    e. Always

12. I am disappointed in my accomplishments I feel I need to accomplish more.

- a. Never
- b. Rarely
- c. Sometimes
- d. Often
- e. Always

13. I am afraid people will find out I do not have the skills or abilities they think I have.

- a. Never
- b. Rarely
- c. Sometimes
- d. Often
- e. Always

14. I am scared I will fail when I accept a new assignment or task even though I'm generally excellent at learning and succeeding with new things.

- a. Never
- b. Rarely
- c. Sometimes
- d. Often
- e. Always

15. When I succeed at something, especially if someone acknowledges my success, I am afraid that I won't be able to continue or repeat the success I have created.

    1. Never

    2. Rarely

    3. Sometimes

    4. Often

    5. Always

16. I tend to devalue the importance of my accomplishments especially when someone recognizes them with praise or compliments.

    6. Never

    7. Rarely

    8. Sometimes

    9. Often

    10. Always

17. I am always comparing myself and my abilities to others and I frequently come out of it feeling like everyone else is smarter or more capable than I am.

    11. Never

    12. Rarely

    13. Sometimes

    14. Often

    15. Always

18. Even if someone else is confident I can do it, I am frequently worried that I will not do well on a new project or test.

16. Never

17. Rarely

18. Sometimes

19. Often

20. Always

19. I do not tell people about my accomplishments until after they've happened because I'm afraid something will go wrong, and it won't go as planned.

21. Never

22. Rarely

23. Sometimes

24. Often

25. Always

20. If I know I'm not going to be somehow "special" or "the best" at something I feel discouraged or upset and have a hard time finding the motivation to even try.

26. Never

27. Rarely

28. Sometimes

29. Often

30. Always

Your Results

If you answered *Never* or *Rarely* to at least 15 of these questions, chances are you do experience some forms of imposter syndrome but not significantly. While you may need to take the time to recover from the bouts of imposter syndrome you are having, chances are these bouts are not causing major setbacks in your life. Instead, they may be more of a nuisance than a full-on disturbance.

If you answered *Rarely* or *Sometimes* to at least 15 of these questions, chances are you do experience imposter syndrome enough that it impacts your productivity and life significantly enough that these symptoms need to be addressed. While it may not impact your day-to-day life, these symptoms could be holding you back in significant ways around meaningful aspects of your life, such as in getting a promotion or taking your relationship to the next level.

If you answered *Sometimes* or *Often* to at least 15 of these questions, chances are you experience imposter syndrome regularly and it affects the quality of your everyday life. You might find you struggle with anxiety at work, in your studies, and in relationships. As well, you might find you have a poor self-image that makes you feel unconfident and overwhelmed in situations where you need to take on or fulfill a responsibility. Healing imposter syndrome will have a significant impact on healing your daily life and giving you the confidence to pursue a more authentic and enjoyable life.

If you answered *Often* or *Always* to at least 15 of these questions, chances are you experience a significant amount of imposter syndrome and feel held back by your symptoms. In addition to affecting the quality of your daily life you might find that you are overwhelmed with anxiety and fear when it comes to taking action to better your life in any way. This overwhelm and anxiety can lead to you holding back or sabotaging your growth and can prevent you from enjoying a quality life. Healing it will give you back the reins in your life by giving you the confidence and courage to pursue the things that matter most to you.

Chapter Summary

Completing the test in this chapter is essential to helping you maintain a deep self-awareness around what your unique experience with imposter syndrome looks like and how it affects your life.

Now you know:

- How deeply you are affected by your imposter syndrome
- What this impact means for your current quality of life
- The level of commitment you will need to overcome this

It's time to start taking action and change your life from the inside out.

PART TWO

REWIRING YOUR BRAIN FOR SUCCESS

CHAPTER 4

Daily Affirmations

"The moment you doubt whether you can fly,
you cease forever to be able to do it."
– James M. Barrie

All throughout your life different messages and statements have been repeated to you in one capacity or another. These could be things that the people around you were saying, or they could be things you say to yourself in response to what is going on in your external or internal world. These statements, as a result of repetition, become a part of your inner dialogue and shape your self-image. When you have had negative messages on repeat your inner dialogue can be critical and harsh. Further, you can have a poor self-image which leads to you having experiences like imposter syndrome.

Affirmations are a deliberate statement you repeat to yourself that is intended to replace the statements you said previously.

These statements are designed to rewire your brain by creating new neural pathways that help you see life with a different perspective. They are excellent for improving self-esteem, creating a positive self-image, and managing or coping with various thoughts you might experience when you are anxious, stressed, depressed, hurting, or experiencing something such as imposter syndrome.

How Do Affirmations Help Imposter Syndrome?

Imposter syndrome can be healed with affirmations that help combat the negative thoughts you have about yourself. The key to ensuring these affirmations work is to use ones that you can reasonably believe to be true, that make you feel better about yourself, and that are easy to repeat. A mistake people frequently make when choosing affirmations is picking ones that they have difficulty internalizing as a belief.

An excellent practice to use that ensures affirmations work as intended is to use laddering affirmations. This means you pick a better belief than the one you have that moves you in the right direction, even if it's not the "final destination" you want to be at. As you affirm it, you look for evidence that this affirmation is true.

Once you have sufficient evidence that your new belief is true you can move on to the next belief that moves you in the right direction. You continue doing this until you reach your desired belief system that allows you to think about yourself, your life, and your circumstances in a positive light.

Below is an example of what belief ladders look like when applied to relationships. In fact, this is the exact belief ladder Ryan from Chapter 1 used when he discovered he had imposter syndrome that was negatively impacting his marriage and family life.

This is what it looked like:

- "I am not worthy of my relationship my partner is going to find out I'm a loser."
  - o Evidence: all of the self-doubt and bad feelings you have been ruminating on.
- "I am not worthy of my relationship but at least I am willing to try."
  - o Evidence: you are reading this book and are willing to find a way to feel worthy of your relationship and be a good partner.
- "I am not worthy of my relationship, but I am hopeful."
  - o Evidence: you have been enforcing the work in this book and you feel hopeful that things will get better and better.
- "I am grateful that I have this relationship it has allowed me to grow as a person."
  - o Evidence: you have gone on a personal journey of healing your imposter syndrome and self-doubt thanks to this relationship.

- "I am enjoying my relationship and am grateful for it."
    - o Evidence: you no longer feel unworthy of the relationship because you have taken action to feel good about your role in it.
- "I am really good at being a loving and considerate partner."
    - o Evidence: you do not hold back, instead you are the partner you want to be because imposter syndrome no longer blocks you.
- "I am worthy of this relationship."
    - o Evidence: you are worthy because you are, and you feel worthy because you have honored yourself and you're healing within your relationship.

As you can see, this was not a direct process from here to there. You did not go from feeling unworthy to worthy in a single bound because, quite frankly, when you feel such a grave amount of self-doubt and uncertainty it's difficult to make that leap. By turning that leap into a journey, however, you get there faster and the results you create are more sustainable.

What Affirmations Can Help You Heal Imposter Syndrome?

You will likely want to create your own affirmations to help you heal your imposter syndrome based on the unique circumstances you are presently experiencing. As you saw above, your affirmations should be based on helping you take one step in the right direction each time. As your new affirmation feels easy to believe and comes naturally to you, you can take the next step.

In case you need some inspiration, here are excellent affirmations for imposter syndrome that can help you come up with your own:

- "I am an asset to any relationship I participate in."
- "Companies benefit by having me on their team."
- "People love being in my company."
- "Regardless of the outcome, I am great at what I do."
- "I know what I am doing."
- "Even if this job doesn't work out, I have a history of people who are happy with my performance."
- "Sometimes I make mistakes, but I can always make things right."
- "People are grateful for the energy I bring to their lives."
- "I bring joy to the lives of those around me."
- "I am enough as I am."

Upon choosing your affirmations ensure you write them down and place them somewhere that you can see them daily. Then, make a point to repeat them out loud to yourself at least three times a day and, as you do, mentally conjure all the evidence you have that proves the new affirmation to be true. This way, you are helping your subconscious mind "upgrade" to the new belief system, and you will have an easier time internalizing and embodying your new chosen beliefs.

Chapter Summary

Affirmations are an incredible way to begin quickly rewiring your subconscious mind by affirming new beliefs that align with the life you desire. In this chapter, you discovered how most people are using affirmations incorrectly and how to implement them properly in your own life.

You also discovered:

- How affirmations actually work in your mind
- What types of affirmations work best
- How to create your own affirmations
- The importance of using a belief ladder to help your mind grow with affirmations
- Excellent affirmations to combat imposter syndrome

Ensure you begin implementing your new affirmations right away. Through the rest of this portion of the book we will go deeper into the psychology of your thoughts and how to take the process of rewiring your thoughts even further. However, this is an essential first step that will help you seek relief rapidly and then cement that change in for good in the coming chapters.

CHAPTER 5

The Power of Positivity

"Any work looks wonderful to me except the one
which I can do." – Ralph Waldo Emerson

Positivity is an extension of affirmations. While affirmations assist you in rewriting the monologue in your brain, positivity helps you completely transform your paradigm and the perspective you have on life. Your paradigm, by the way, is the "fixed level" of belief you have about life. This is the inner compass that guides you back to what is comfortable after everything you experience in the world. A great example of a paradigm in action is when someone test out a new diet or exercise routine to better their health. They may be enthusiastic and fully committed to this new program for a couple of weeks then it falls off and they are back to the same habits they had in the first place. This 'baseline' is the paradigm. Imposter syndrome is a part of your 'baseline.'

Executing the power of positivity is an excellent way to elevate your baseline beyond imposter syndrome and similarly self-sabotaging thought processes while also giving you a greater connection to your life. There are several steps you can take to help implement more positivity in your everyday life. Incorporating these steps into your daily routine is an excellent way to allow positivity to seep into all areas of your life and facilitate change in your world.

Below are five steps you can take to help you become a more positive person and rewire your brain in a way that naturally eliminates imposter syndrome *without* masking its presence or making you feel like you have to suppress it to thrive.

Acts Of Kindness

Kindness is an action that elevates your experience as well as the experience of someone else. It has long been understood that if you want to improve your mood or feel better about yourself, do something kind for someone else. This could be volunteering, paying for someone's coffee, picking up groceries for a friend, helping someone carry their bags into the house, babysitting or pet sitting for a friend, helping someone clean their home, sending a greeting card, or anything else that represents kindness to someone else.

Alicia, who I introduced you to in Chapter 1, used acts of kindness as a way to help herself move through her imposter syndrome at the law firm. By being kind to her fellow partners she felt *good* working at the same level as them. Over time, her sense of belonging grew, and she realized that she was more than worthy and capable of fulfilling her role as partner. Before she knew it, she was excited and proud of her position and imposter syndrome was a thing of the past.

When you commit an act of kindness you are engaged in doing something special and meaningful for someone else. The realization that your effort results in someone else feeling better can help you feel better, too. One study done by PLOS ONE proved that random acts of kindness actually do improve overall mental health, which includes relieving symptoms of irritating or discouraging mental experiences like imposter syndrome.

A key to getting the most out of your acts of kindness is to do them frequently but do not do them for the purpose of gaining anything in return. For example, do not babysit your sister's kids in exchange for her washing your car. While this is certainly kind, it is more of a negotiation than a genuine act of kindness that elevates your mood. Instead, focus on the small acts that you can engage in, often without any recognition, and do them frequently. These don't have to be significant to be worthy, it can be as simple as holding doors open for people or watching their dog while they run into a shop.

The more you engage in acts of kindness, the more opportunities you will see to engage in further acts of kindness. As it becomes a part of your personality you will find it easier to see yourself with a positive self-image as a person who does good deeds for others and is therefore a positive member of society. Through this, you are likely to experience relief from imposter syndrome and other concerns.

Giving Thanks

Gratitude is frequently referenced when positive thinking is called for, and for good reason. Giving thanks publicly or openly is a great way to express your gratitude to others for who they are or how they have helped you. However, it is not the only way to experience gratitude. Even quiet moments of gratitude expressed to yourself, or your journal is a great way to focus on the wonderful things you have in life and the blessings you have received. As you teach your mind to focus on things you are grateful for it becomes easier for you to think about all of the positive things you have going on in your life. This, in turn, becomes a habit that replaces the worry and self-doubt that frequently accompany imposter syndrome.

Beyond helping you think better thoughts, gratitude has been shown to help you feel more focused and grounded, be more present, and be resilient against life's challenges. This means even when imposter syndrome does spring up, you will feel more confident about managing its symptoms and creating relief for yourself.

There are three wonderful ways you can tap into the entirety of gratitude. The first two we already briefly discussed: verbally giving thanks to the people in your life and quietly doing it in a gratitude journal or thought practice.

The third way of expressing gratitude is one that also helps you deepen your connection to the present moment and experience as much joy in the "here and now" as possible. This is also the best one for overcoming imposter syndrome in the moment it strikes. That is: finding gratitude in *this moment*. My friend Barbara actually taught me about the importance of this form of gratitude when she was reflecting on how she felt like an imposter after the birth of her first son. She explained to me that by slowing down and finding gratitude in each moment she was able to elevate herself from these feelings of self-doubt and fear and find reasons to simply enjoy this moment.

You can practice right now by setting this book down for a moment, observing the room around you, and expressing gratitude for the different things you have that support your wellbeing. Perhaps you give gratitude for the seat you are on, the floor under your feet, and the socks or shoes on your feet. You might express gratitude for the air you're breathing, the book you are holding, or the device allowing you to access the book.

This similar process can be executed in moments when imposter syndrome strikes, too. For example, say you are in a meeting, and it strikes. In that moment, you would pause for a moment and focus instead on how grateful you are for your job, cowork-ers, managers, the tools you use to complete your job, and the way your job pays for the things you care about like your home, vehicle, and nice meals. This shift in focus will drastically change the way you think about life and help you head-off im-poster syndrome the moment it strikes.

Enjoying The Small Things

People as a whole are equipped with a mental process called "negativity bias." This means we are literally wired to be nega-tive toward the world and ourselves, which is the perfect breed-ing ground for issues like imposter syndrome to arise in the first place. A great way to combat negativity bias, which often causes us to dwell on things that make us worry or doubtful, is to dwell on positive things instead.

Chris, the gentleman who was struggling at university in chap-ter 1, used this method to help himself enjoy university more. For so long, his entire academic experience had been about eve-ryone else. He was so busy proving he was worthy and capable of having the opportunity he'd made for himself that he forgot to stop and *enjoy* being in university. This is where much of his partying behavior came from: rebelling against the high stress he felt he was under. When he realized he was allowed to slow down and enjoy university and the process of being an aca-demic student, he found ways beyond drinking and partying. Through that, his approach to studying became more balanced and he reclaimed his great grades and graduated near the top of his class.

This might involve dwelling on the delight of having clean dishes to eat with because your spouse washed them or dwelling in the joy of having all the office supplies you need to complete your job. You might dwell on something kind someone said to you and how it made you feel, or on how you felt realizing that you did a job well done on a certain task you were worried about.

You can dwell at random on the enjoyment you gain from the little things, or you can make a deliberate practice out of this. Your deliberate practice could involve you sitting down at the same time every day and picking two or three wonderful elements of your day and simply dwelling on them. Think about how they made you feel, how much you enjoyed them, how they added to the quality of your day and life, and anything else they created for you. Keep dwelling until you feel your entire mood shift.

A Daily Journal

There are many ways to keep a journal, but if your goal is to boost your positivity an excellent way to do so is to keep a positivity journal. Your positivity journal is a daily journal that you write *only* positive things in. You must not dwell on any emotions your imposter syndrome created or any negative feelings that have sprung forth in your life. While you do not want to bypass those feelings, the goal of this journal is to remind you that other feelings and perspectives exist, too.

Each morning, sit down with your positivity journal and write all of the things you feel great about. This can include your gratitude list. You can even get present and begin writing about how wonderful you feel in your life with all the different things around you in that moment or reflect on a positive memory for how you acquired something in your environment. The idea is to get as positive as possible and create an attitude where you feel good.

Each night, sit down with your positivity journal and write all of the positive things that happened to you that day. Share positive stories, things that lifted your mood, and experiences that made you feel better. Never write about a bad mood you had that was improved, instead write about the improvement. For example, rather than saying "I was in a bad mood until Sharon from accounting brought me a coffee, how kind!" simply say "Sharon from accounting brought me a coffee and it was a wonderful gift, I was so grateful!" Keeping it entirely focused on positive thinking allows you to truly make a habit out of seeing the greatness in all of life and benefitting from all that it has to offer.

Once you have filled out your positivity journal, or whenever you are feeling particularly low with imposter syndrome and self-doubt, read through your journal and remember all the wonderful things that have happened in your life. This is a great way to remind yourself that even though there *are* hard times and sometimes you *do* feel badly about yourself, you are a wonderful person that is living a wonderful life.

Looking For The Silver Lining

Finally, it truly is a gift to be able to look for the silver lining in any situation you encounter in life. Looking for the silver lining isn't about pretending everything is hunky dory and that you only ever experience good things in life. Instead, it's about finding balance in the harder aspects of life and realizing that even in the depths of trouble or difficulty you can find something to give you hope.

There are two ways you can look for the silver linings in your life: candidly throughout the day and deliberately each night when you do your journaling and gratitude reflections.

Candidly, you can pause anytime you find yourself facing something you do not enjoy and take a moment to look for at least three reasons why this might be positive. For example, if you just left a meeting at work where you were informed you would be taking a new project and you now feel imposter syndrome rising, you can think about three benefits of doing this project. Perhaps it gives you the opportunity to learn new skills, collaborate with new people, and practice developing confidence in yourself.

Daily, you can sit down and pick out two or three parts of your day that didn't go as hoped or that presented bad news you were unhappy to receive. With each one, look for three reasons you can be grateful or hopeful in these scenarios. Write them down or say them out loud and let yourself genuinely acknowledge the good that can come of each situation. This practice will teach you to see that not everything is black-and-white and that you can find good even in the hard parts of your life.

Chapter Summary

Positivity is a life-changing mindset that anyone can foster. By appropriating these activities into your daily routine, you can provide yourself with a direct route to deepening your positive mindset and uprooting the negative one that feeds your thoughts of self-doubt and self-criticism.

In this chapter you learned five important practices:

- Acts of kindness
- Giving thanks
- Enjoying the small things
- Keeping a journal
- Looking for the silver lining

These practices work through a system known as *compound positivity*. This means that the more you complete these practices the more your positivity will compound *and* the more benefit you will gain from them. Over time, imposter syndrome will cease to exist because it simply has no reason to.

CHAPTER 6

Adopting A Growth Mindset

"I have written 11 books, but each time I think
"uh oh, they're going to find me out now."
– Maya Angelou

As you can now tell, imposter syndrome seriously implicates your ability to pursue personal and professional goals and take significant steps of growth in your life. I'm a firm believer that people with imposter syndrome have a growth mindset *naturally*. The reason for that is: you wouldn't continually put yourself in situations that create imposter syndrome if you didn't. Further, you wouldn't even care to heal your imposter syndrome if you weren't already committed to growing beyond what you have already created in life to achieve even more. If you had a fixed mindset, the alternative to a growth mindset, you'd be "stuck in your ways." You wouldn't crave growth, expansion, or any circumstance that would make you uncomfortable. You would be happily perched in your comfort zone and unwilling to move beyond it.

One way you can combat imposter syndrome is by adopting a growth mindset *on purpose.* In other words, rather than merely holding onto the internal hope that things will get better, take action to deliberately put yourself out there and act on your desire for growth. Reading this book is an excellent start, but there is plenty more you can do to move beyond your comfort zone and heal your imposter syndrome in the process.

When you concentrate on creating a growth mindset on purpose, you also focus on accepting the natural experiences that come with growth: like mistakes, failure, and setbacks. This means that, rather than feeling blindsided by them, you're looking forward to them. You anticipate them, and you are ready for them. You have been working on training your mindset to respond to them in a healthy, growth-oriented way, and you are prepared to overcome them when they arise.

As you focus on your growth mindset, it is essential to focus both on the actions of growth and the mentality behind the actions. This way, as you take bold steps, you *also* create a mental atmosphere that favors expansion. This way, no matter how things play out, you will be cheering yourself on and celebrating your wins.

Alicia, Chris, and Ryan are all excellent examples of fostering a growth mindset to overcome the imposter syndrome they were facing. Each of them chose to embrace their imposter syndrome and find ways to overcome it rather than succumb to their feelings and give up, as many often do. My friend Patricia is an excellent example of the power of a growth mindset, too.

Patricia was a student at a prominent beauty school in Canada, where she studied special FX makeup for theatre and movie characters. For the first year of her studies, Patricia felt entirely out of place. She rapidly realized that her unique brand of creativity was not "normal" in school and did everything she could to fit in with what others had been doing. While her makeup skills were phenomenal, they didn't stand out above her peers.

Finally, one day she talked with her instructor and admitted that her studies weren't what she expected they would be. That's when her instructor assured her that her creativity was welcomed and that if she had new and exciting ways of trying things, this was *precisely* the time to test them out! When she embraced a growth mindset and took action to implement her unique brand of creativity, her skills exploded. She excelled beyond what was expected of her, rose to the top of her class, and landed several prestigious roles even long before she graduated from the school. Because Patricia was unwilling to give up and decided to be honest and lean into growth, a world of opportunities opened up for her. This is far better than the alternative could have been: which would have been her dropping out, pursuing a practical degree, and finding a job she didn't enjoy just because that's what she was "supposed to do."

While there are countless ways to cultivate a growth mindset, I have a simple six-step process I like to use that makes it incredibly simple. You will likely still face up against fear, discomfort, and other symptoms of imposter syndrome, but you will already have the tools to overcome those experiences as they arise. Thus, it is the perfect way to get yourself moving and create the desired outcome *without* expecting yourself to simply "deal with" your symptoms.

Begin By Identifying Your Current Mindset

The first step to cultivating your growth mindset is to figure out what your current mindset looks like. While I'm confident you have a growth mindset, you might be trapped in a fixed mindset. Alternatively, you might have a growth mindset but *act* like you have a fixed mindset because you are afraid of fear.

How do you know which mindset you have? Look at your thoughts. A growth mindset says, "things can get better, and I can grow through this." A fixed mindset says, "nothing will get better, and this is the best it gets for me." Since you're here reading this book, I'd assume you're experiencing thoughts aligned with the former statement.

Still, you are struggling with acting on your desire to improve things, which is why you need to assess your mindset even deeper. The better you understand your present thoughts and how they affect your willingness and ability to take action, the easier it will be to combat these thoughts and step beyond your comfort zone despite their best effort to keep you safe.

Here are some questions to help you dig into your present mindset and better understand how it is shaping your experience:

1. When you think about trying something new, what specific thoughts surface?
2. When you think about things you've already accomplished, what are your thoughts like? How do you explain these successes to yourself?
3. When you think about your success compared to other people's success, what are your exact thoughts?
4. When you think about your abilities compared to other people's abilities, what are your exact thoughts?
5. When you think about your life goals, what thoughts do you have about yourself, your abilities, and your likelihood of reaching these goals?

If these questions bring up further insight for you, continue writing. The idea is to get it all out on paper so you can see *exactly* how your present thoughts affect your action. The deeper you go with this practice, the easier it will be to prepare yourself for the various thoughts that will surface to thwart your progress and keep you in your comfort zone.

Learn Something New

Armed with your detailed description of your present mindset, you can begin to take the next significant step in cultivating your growth mindset, which involves learning something new. The excellent part about this process is you can choose to learn *anything*. It can be related to your profession, or it can be completely separate. Hobbies, crafts, sports, recipes, there are plenty of new things you can learn that will help you practice implementing a growth mindset.

You can approach picking your new thing in two ways either learn one thing at a time to keep yourself focused and paced, or you can select two things. The reason behind selecting two things is you can choose one that is little to no pressure and one that has a little more pressure behind it. For example, you might learn to sew and how to perform a new skill at work. This way, you can practice implementing your new growth mindset skills in a variety of situations, and it has a positive impact on your work life, which tends to be the aspect of life where imposter syndrome can become the most problematic.

Be Willing To Make Mistakes

One of the biggest fears people struggling with imposter syndrome have, is the fear of making a mistake because they fear being perceived as a fraud. If you are afraid of people thinking you are fake or that you secretly are incapable of fulfilling their expectations of you, the idea of making a mistake can feel mildly traumatizing. You might find you are so turned off by making mistakes that, even upon trying something new, you move at a plodding pace to perfect each step, so you do not make any errors.

The idea of trying something new is creating opportunities to make mistakes and develop resiliency around the mistakes you've made. While you may never feel *good* about making mistakes, you can desensitize yourself to them by creating a positive mindset that fosters opportunity and optimism around mistakes.

In other words, rather than feeling like a mistake exposes you as a fraud, you can learn to see that mistakes are positive evidence that you are growing and trying new things and that you have unique opportunities to learn even more. The reality is: everyone makes mistakes. Even the most successful people in the world make them on a regular basis. Accepting yourself as you are and using mistakes as an opportunity to learn more is a great way to align yourself with growth rather than fear.

Be Kind To Yourself

In addition to adjusting your mindset around what mistakes are and becoming willing to make mistakes in the first place, you need to lean into step four which is to be kind to yourself deliberately. Often, our fear of mistakes comes not from the people around us but from how we treat ourselves. Our entire imposter syndrome complex can come from the way we treat ourselves.

When you punish yourself for making mistakes or getting things wrong, and continually tell yourself you are a fraud and do not deserve what you have, it's only natural that you're going to feel anxious and afraid of trying new things. However, when you make a point of being kind to yourself and celebrating your efforts and soothing your worries, it becomes a lot less overwhelming to try new things or make mistakes in the process.

As you go through the journey of uncovering your growth mindset, focus on the affirmations you made earlier. You might even take it a step further by creating new ones for your growth mindset journey.

These affirmations might be:

- "I learn from my mistakes."
- "I am allowed to be a beginner."
- "It is safe for me to grow from this."
- "I am completely normal for needing time to figure it out."
- "I am still worthy even when I make a mistake."
- "I am still capable even if it takes me time to learn."

These affirmations are excellent for combatting the harsh and unkind thoughts you might be engaging with when you make mistakes with your current mindset.

Look To Others For Examples

Another excellent way to cultivate a growth mindset is to look to others for examples. Because you are facing imposter syndrome, I suspect you have already looked to others in a capacity that leads to comparison. Therefore, I don't want you to look to others for an example of what is possible for you. Instead, I want you to use other people to create confidence in the "less perfect" parts of yourself.

For example, James Dyson, creator of the famous Dyson vacuum, failed at creating his vacuum 5,126 times before finally making one that worked. That is a hefty commitment to figuring it out, and I can only imagine the resilience he must have developed along the way. While you are unlikely to fail that many times at the skill you are learning, it is an excellent reminder that even the most successful people fail. Look for examples in your life of people achieving incredible things and who regularly fail, struggle, and face up against self-doubt and self-criticism. You'll be surprised to learn how common this is! You might also discover new ways of handling these doubts and thoughts when they surface, so they don't take root and stop you from getting into action.

Set Realistic Goals For Yourself

Finally, it is essential to set realistic goals for yourself. I think that you can achieve anything you set your mind to. I believe it because I believe *anyone* can achieve anything they set their mind to. However, when healing something as intrusive as imposter syndrome, jumping straight into massive goals may not be the best idea. Instead, this might lead to more triggers that leave you feeling even more like a fraud.

It is better to focus on goals that are more realistic and believable from the start so you can build the skills needed to reach those larger goals. In these smaller, more realistic goals, you can develop resiliency, courage, a growth mindset, kindness, confidence, and other mindsets you need to help you succeed.

A great way to set your goals so they are worth achieving *and* realistic is to choose your most significant life goal and place it at the top of a sheet of paper. Then, break it down into the smaller milestone goals you'd need to achieve to succeed at that goal. Once you have it broken down you can start at the first goal and use that to cultivate your growth mindset and all the skills you need to succeed. As you become more empowered through each successful goal, you'll find yourself making strides toward your larger purpose and feeling more confident in it and yourself.

Chapter Summary

A growth mindset is an essential tool for anyone seeking to live a high quality of life. I know you have one because you are here learning how to overcome imposter syndrome. I also understand that your imposter syndrome is the direct result of you trying to grow and become a better version of yourself.

Now you know it, too. You also know that:

- Working with your growth mindset is better than working against it
- You can adopt a growth mindset by developing your self-awareness
- Learning something new helps deliberately trigger imposter syndrome
- Once it's activated, you can practice seeking opportunities and being kind to yourself
- The importance of setting realistic goals for yourself

The more you put yourself in these situations, the more resilient you will become. Further, you create the opportunity to become used to being a 'beginner' or being in the learning stages of new skills. As a result, you find confidence, and comfort in this role and it stops feeling so triggering.

CHAPTER 7

Practicing Visualization

"I have a very vibrant imposter syndrome that goes on throughout most of my life, but nothing more than when someone has to put a hat on me or some kind of sash and go, 'We're giving you this certificate." – Robin Ince

Visualization is a phenomenal practice that has shown impressive promise in helping people take control of their minds and succeed in reaching their goals. According to researchers, visualization works because our brains interpret the imagery in our minds as a real-life experience.

This is why, when you get tangled up with your thoughts caused by imposter syndrome, they begin to feel so real. As you fantasize about people discovering you're a fraud or you make a mistake and everyone realizing you are not worthy or capable, you create an experience in your mind that causes your brain to believe this has actually happened. Thus, you experience real fear and anxiety as if you have already been 'caught.' The more frequently you engage in these fears, the stronger they become which is why the longer your imposter syndrome goes un-treated the more difficult it is to change your mind. Fortunately, your mind is *always* changeable, no matter how bad your symp-toms become.

A great way to change it is to use visualization. Just as this prac-tice has helped you worsen your symptoms; it can also help you improve them. By deliberately visualizing yourself experienc-ing confidence, self-assurance, self-validation, success, worthi-ness, and capability, you create the experience within yourself that this is true. At the same time, you create new neural path-ways that prime your mind to move your body in a way that agrees with this being your authentic experience. Over time, your imposter syndrome begins to fade as you feel better.

There are plenty of techniques you can use to reinforce visuali-zation and gain the most out of this practice. In this chapter, we will go through all five and end with a guided visualization practice you can follow to help you see your success in detail.

Write With Your Senses

The late self-help author Bob Proctor frequently spoke about how writing engages your thoughts, and your thoughts can change your life. Writing is an excellent way to immerse your-self in the visualization process, especially if you are someone who does not thrive in meditation. Through this practice, you put pen to paper and deliberately write your desired outcome while intentionally infusing all of your senses into the experience.

For example, when combatting imposter syndrome, you would write about how it feels to have overcome it. You should begin your statement with "I am so grateful now that…" and end it with a paragraph about how it feels to no longer struggle with imposter syndrome. You can talk about how your emotions feel in your newfound confidence, what your thoughts are like, how your body feels when you are in formerly triggering situations, what you hear from the people around you, and how life looks. If your recovery from imposter syndrome means you are in new situations that involve smell or taste, include those details as well.

You can write a detailed paragraph as often as three times a day to help prepare your mind for a world where you no longer experience imposter syndrome. You can even write this paragraph out immediately before getting into a scenario where your imposter syndrome is traditionally triggered, such as a meeting or a first date. The more you write it out, the better. This repetition will help you cement the new visualization into your mind and make a lasting change in how you perceive yourself and how you experience different situations.

Imagine The Emotion

One way to appropriate your visualization is to focus on emotion. Your brain is particularly attached to emotional experiences, which is why anything that causes fear seems to linger. This is the same reason why situations that make you feel especially happy, or comforting become attractive, and you want to continually engage in those emotions more frequently.

As you engage in your visualization of a life free of imposter syndrome, focus on the emotions associated with the outcome. How does it feel? What comes up for you? Do feelings change in different situations? Do they change throughout one situation? Imagine what it would be like to go through one complete experience without experiencing even one moment of imposter syndrome. How would you feel when it was over?

Going into emotional detail about your visualization helps your brain internalize it and take it more seriously. The more you can infuse feeling into it, the more your brain will favor this visual. If you can dwell on it enough that you focus on the positive emotion of overcoming imposter syndrome *more* than on the negative emotion of imposter syndrome itself, you might find yourself overcoming it significantly faster.

Visualize The Setbacks

As we discussed in the previous chapter, setbacks are inevitable. Mistakes happen, and the best thing you can do is learn to accept them. One way to set yourself ahead is to deliberately visualize the setbacks you are likely to face in the process of overcoming imposter syndrome. These are the mistakes, feedback, and other circumstances that would arise and cause you to generally feel panicked, doubtful, and fearful due to your imposter syndrome.

In your visualizations, imagine those triggering situations until you begin to feel the familiar feelings of panic, doubt, and fear. Then, start using your affirmations. Finally, encourage yourself to become curious and visualize how that situation might play out differently. Consider how people might *actually* feel or react to you, what the situation would be like, and what the realistic outcome would be.

As you play the scene to the end with your new visualization methods of realizing that your biggest fears are unlikely to come true, you essentially eliminate all reasons for being afraid of that situation in the first place. In the end, you neutralize the emotional experience that comes from having a setback and create space for you to feel calmer and more balanced when these do arise.

Expand Your Knowledge

Occasionally, you may visualize your desired outcome and realize you do not know what it would look like if you approached a situation in any other way. Sometimes this is why you are having trouble in the first place. Because you cannot imagine something going well, you only have the skills to make it go poorly. Thus, you become panicked. In these cases, a great way to overcome your fear and deepen your visualization is to expand your knowledge.

You expand your knowledge by observing or asking how other people overcome doubt, panic, and fear. As you discover this new information, you pay close attention to the ones who respond in a way that would serve you best. Then, you visualize yourself responding in that same way. By seeing yourself react and respond to different situations in a healthier, more balanced way in your visualization process, you create the belief that you can and the pathway to learning the skills so that you *do* respond better.

Make Time For Reflection

Whenever you visualize, it is a good idea to make time to reflect on the visualization after. Anytime you engage in visualization, a ton of new information will surface, even if you are visualizing the same thing, you had previously. Each time, you want to jot that information down and use it to assist you with growing closer to your desired outcome.

For example, imagine yourself going through a meeting at work without experiencing any imposter syndrome. Even when someone delegates a task to you that generally elicits fear, you respond with gratitude and excitement rather than panic and self-doubt. You are genuinely eager to learn from this new skill and grow with it.

As you visualize this, you might notice in the background you have feelings surface that doubts your ability ever to feel this way. Beneath it all, you might feel like this visualization is "hopeful dreaming," and the reality is that no matter how hard you try, you will never overcome the thoughts and feelings that keep you struggling. This is an important note to jot down as it illuminates a belief you have that will continue to hold you back until you heal it.

Rather than trying to force yourself to believe that you can heal your imposter syndrome, then you would go back to the belief-shifting process from Chapter 4 and gradually elevate yourself into your new belief system. For example, you would begin by believing that you can at least feel less terrified when a project is delegated to you. In addition to feeling panicked and doubtful, you also feel hopeful that you can use this as an opportunity to grow.

Another realization people frequently have during their visualization process is that their desired outcome doesn't necessarily feel the way they anticipated it would. For example, you might assume that overcoming imposter syndrome means you're always going to feel excited, energized, and ready to tackle every new task that comes your way. While this might be true occasionally, it is more likely that you will feel a more peaceful sense of joy, gratitude, and confidence. That's because once something has been appropriated into your reality, the novelty wears off. Rather than being exciting and newsworthy it simply becomes an everyday fact of life.

When you can begin to see and experience life from that calm, balanced approach, you know you've made massive strides in healing your imposter syndrome.

Guided Visualization To Overcome Imposter Syndrome

If you can close your eyes and meditate for some time, you can walk yourself through a guided visualization practice that helps you overcome your imposter syndrome. This guided visualization practice should be done for about ten minutes twice daily: once in the morning and once at night. If you use the positivity journal I mentioned in an earlier chapter, this would be an excellent addition to that daily practice.

To do this guided visualization practice, you first want to set your space up for it. Begin by creating a comfortable spot to sit with your feet planted firmly on the floor or your legs crossed if you will be seated on the floor. Ensure you are comfortable, and warm enough and that nothing will distract you from your practice. You might also choose to play meditation music from your preferred streaming service to prevent you from getting distracted while also helping you feel more relaxed.

Once you have everything arranged, read through the script one time. Then, close your eyes and imagine yourself going through the script. Imagine all of the details the script calls on to help you deeply engage with your visualization practice. When you are done, please open your eyes and take a few moments to reflect on how it felt, what you discovered, and any information that could help you improve your imposter syndrome and feel more confident and grounded.

Begin by closing your eyes and taking three slow, deep breaths through your nose and out through your mouth. After the third breath, allow your mouth to gently close and focus on letting your breath to resume its natural rhythm, whatever that looks like for you.

When you feel calm and comfortably focused on your breath, recall a time when you felt imposter syndrome come up for you. Think about where you were, what you were doing, and what created this feeling.

Then, think about how this feeling felt for you. What thoughts did you have? What did you feel in your body? What did you do as a result? How did you feel about your reaction to your emotions?

Let yourself dwell on this image for a moment.

Then, imagine yourself picking up a remote controller and "rewinding" the scene back to the beginning. Visualize that same experience unfolding. Only this time imagine that you felt calm, confident, and assured. Imagine you responded to the situation in a way that made you feel proud.

What would that look like? How would that feel? What thoughts would you be having? How would you respond? How would you feel about the response itself?

Once you reach the end of the scene affirm to yourself: "That is me. I am that. I respond with calm, confidence, and assurance. All is well. I am capable."

Focus on your breath again for a few moments before bringing your awareness back into the room and awakening yourself from this experience.

Chapter Summary

Are you amazed by the truth that your brain cannot tell the difference between what you visualize and what you actually experience? Visualization is a powerful tool that many people are entirely unaware of.

Here are the six visualization tools you learned in this chapter:

- Writing down your visualization helps mobilize it in your mind
- Imagining the emotion enables you to internalize your visualization
- Visualizing setbacks helps desensitize you to the fear of them

- Expanding your knowledge helps you overcome uncertainty
- Reflecting on your visualizations builds self-awareness
- Guided visualization can help you internalize your desires through meditation

Regardless of what your chosen method for visualization is, you have now learned plenty of ways to internalize your desires and expand your ability to use visualization to overcome imposter syndrome.

CHAPTER 8

Positive Self-Talk and
Imposter Syndrome

"A joyful life is an individual creation that
cannot be copied from a recipe."
– Mihaly Csikszentmihalyi

B y now, you understand the power your inner monologue can have on your psyche and how substantially it can affect your thoughts, feelings, and behaviors. So far, you are using affirmations effectively. You may even be seeing a payoff already by refocusing your mind on positive statements anytime you find yourself being faced with imposter syndrome.

Now, we will take it a step deeper by digging into a common therapeutic practice that dives beyond statements and into the complete inner monologue you have with yourself. This practice is called cognitive behavioral therapy or CBT.

What Is CBT?

Whether you realize it or not, your thoughts are constantly assessing and addressing the world around you. These thoughts operate like conversations between your inner world and your outer experience. When you tune into these thoughts, you'll get a more robust understanding of what is going on in your inner world and how it may be contributing to experiences like imposter syndrome.

As you gain a deeper-level awareness of these thoughts, you will recognize that they play out in a cyclical pattern. You will also identify an opportunity to interrupt the cycle and create a new thought pattern that throws imposter syndrome off its tracks and enables you to lean into a healthier and more supportive thought process. This may be accompanied by a shift in your actions, as well, to help you appropriate the change.

Similar to the gradual improvement process I've described earlier, this will enable you to experience a shift from the anxious thought pattern triggered by imposter syndrome and instead focus on a calmer and more balanced one. Over time, this new thought pattern becomes habitual and you are no longer triggered toward the habitual thoughts of imposter syndrome.

Mindfulness For Identifying Thought Cycles

To effectively implement CBT, you first need to understand what your problematic thought cycles are. If you have dealt with imposter syndrome for a prolonged period, you likely have many triggers that cause you to experience the symptoms of imposter syndrome.

Regardless of how long you've experienced these symptoms before, it's possible that you have not yet identified the entire thought processes happening around your inner self-talk during a bout of imposter syndrome. For CBT to be most effective, you must notice the overwhelming thought *and* the thoughts surrounding it. This is how you will identify the entirety of your imposter syndrome and find the best opportunities to change your thinking when it strikes completely.

The easiest way to dig into the core of your thought process and map out the entire experience is to keep a notepad and pen with you or create a separate note in your phone specifically to track your thoughts. Whenever a negative thought related to imposter syndrome arises, you will stop and write that thought down.

If you are unaware of what your imposter syndrome thoughts are, begin by writing a list of thoughts you generally have that accompany bouts of it. A simple moment spent reflecting on the thoughts that come over you most, and lead to the most problems, will suffice.

Remember, these are the thoughts that sound like:

- "I got lucky, and I didn't deserve this."
- "I am not worthy of having this, and they made a mistake."

- "I didn't deserve the success I received."
- "They are going to find out I'm actually incapable of this."
- "I don't want to get 'found out' for being a fraud."

Once you have a list of what your most common problematic thoughts are, you can keep this nearby and make a point to become mindful of whenever these thoughts surface. The idea is to develop a sense of self-awareness that allows you to consciously notice the moment these thoughts start or as close to that first moment as possible. Because you are now deliberately looking for these thoughts, you will automatically start paying attention to them and taking inventory when they surface.

Then, when they do surface, you will take out your notebook, write down the thought, and jot down the answer to the following questions:

- What was happening that triggered this thought?
- What was my first thought after that happened?
- What was my thought before the thought I'm having?
- What thought am I currently having?
- What would my next thought typically be if I hadn't stopped to write this down?

Then, you can put your notebook down. Over the next several minutes, remain mindful of your thoughts and jot down any further thoughts that surface. The idea is to get as much of it on paper as possible to see the entirety of your problematic thought cycle.

It is a good idea to repeat this process for a few days so you can get your imposter syndrome cycle written on paper a few times over. This way, you can compare the cycles and notice recurring problematic thoughts.

Preparing For Your Moment Of Interruption

Once you have assessed yourself and identified what your problematic thought cycle is, it's time to prepare for your moment of disruption. Your moment of disruption is your opportunity to "hijack" your brain *back* from imposter syndrome by observing your thought pattern and looking for opportunities to disprove it.

When we get carried away with emotional thought patterns, we experience what is called an "emotional hijacking." This means your brain becomes so triggered by the thought process you are having that you cannot separate yourself from it and align yourself with truth or reality. Instead, you are convinced that the fears you are facing are "true."

The experience of being emotionally hijacked can be particularly frustrating because you are likely fully aware of the misinformation *outside* of the hijacking, but as it's happening, it feels authentic. You begin to act as if your thoughts are accurate and, in many cases, can sabotage yourself and your life experience as a result.

To prevent emotional hijackings from occurring, you want to observe the thought patterns you've been writing down and identify areas where you are continually being taken over by false beliefs. The idea is to disprove these and begin to believe differently when you are not emotionally charged so that in triggering moments, you have a fundamental belief system to lean back on and support you with preventing emotional hijackings in action.

Begin by observing your thought patterns and, on a separate piece of paper, writing out every false thought you experience during a bout of imposter syndrome. Place a star or highlight ones that you repeatedly have, as these are especially problematic and will become the most important ones for you to target with CBT.

Once you have a clear view of what is going on, begin writing next to each thought the truth as it is, not as your mind suggests it is when you feel triggered.

For example, yours might look like this:

- ~~I am not good enough for this job.~~ *I was good enough to get hired.*
- ~~My boss even criticized me.~~ *She gave me advice on how to improve.*
- ~~She thinks I'm terrible at my job.~~ *She sees my potential and wants to help.*

- ~~I'm probably going to get fired.~~ *I have done nothing to deserve being fired.*
- ~~No matter what I do, I'm not good enough.~~ *I keep getting better every day.*
- ~~Why do I even bother trying?~~ *I can choose to keep trying and getting better.*

By writing these statements that identify the truth, rather than your triggered thoughts, you create space to see things differently. This allows you to see that because there is an alternative to your current thought process, there is reason to believe that your imposter syndrome is not inherently true. Thus, you destroy the foundation upon which all those false critical beliefs were built. You can rely on this shift to help you in moments when you are actively being triggered by imposter syndrome.

Reframing Your Thoughts: In Action

The next step is to reframe your thoughts in action. This is where you get to have the most significant impact on your imposter syndrome because you are now changing your thoughts in the very moment that they would have previously hijacked you. It is essential first to set your expectations around this experience, as you are unlikely to do it perfectly the first time. You might attempt to shift your thoughts many times before the new belief system takes root and stops imposter syndrome in its tracks.

Reframing your thoughts into action requires you to lean on the truth you identified in the previous step and actively replace thoughts related to imposter syndrome as they arise. For example, the next time your boss criticizes your work, rather than spiraling out of control with thoughts of unworthiness, you will focus on recognizing it as an opportunity to receive and implement constructive feedback.

To shift your thoughts in action, you will use the truth-based thoughts you identified previously, similarly to how you use affirmations. Instead of repeating the same statement over and over, you will have a back-and-forth dialogue with your inner voice. Your goal is to disprove it and identify the truth, which is generally a lot kinder than the reality the voice inside is feeding you.

If you cannot remember the truths, you wrote previously, or if you find yourself in a new situation facing up against new thoughts, the best question is: "Is this true?"

For example, the inner conversation could look like this:

- "My spouse picked me because I acted like I am better than I actually am."
- "Is this true? No, they have seen me at some of my lowest points."
- "Maybe they wanted to leave but felt obligated to stay."
- "Is this true? No, they tell me they love me every day."

- "Maybe they say that out of obligation but don't really believe it."
- "Is this true? No, they put effort into having a good relationship with me."
- "Am I really an imposter in my relationship, or am I having a hard time?"
- "Maybe I am just having a hard time and am being unfair to myself."
- "I can choose kinder thoughts than this. What would that look like?"
- "I don't like how I acted in a certain situation, but I know I can do better. I will reflect on it and be a better spouse, because ultimately, I am worthy of my partner."

Engaging in this back-and-forth dialogue with yourself by discrediting catastrophizing or black-and-white thinking and replacing it with more forgiving thoughts is a great way to derail the negative thought cycle and get on board with something more thoughtful. The kinder thoughts are also more productive. They either save you time by eliminating unnecessary emotional spirals, or they assist you with discovering newer and healthier ways of approaching circumstances you might actually wish to change in your life.

Regardless of whether the circumstance needs to be accepted or changed, you need to be in a positive frame of mind do it. Through CBT, you can shift your mindset from a negative one to a positive one, thereby allowing yourself to take control of the situation, improve your thoughts, latch onto a growth mind-set, and experience better outcomes.

Continually Rewiring Your Brain With CBT

When it comes to something as complex as imposter syndrome, there are often many beliefs and thought processes in the background that accompany this experience. You might also find that many triggers cause these different thought processes to unfold. Another experience people often have is realizing that their imposter syndrome affects them more than they thought it did. For example, you might be reading this book because you experience imposter syndrome at work. Still, as you continue to do the work to heal your imposter syndrome, you might discover that you also experience it in your relationships.

As each awareness of a new thought cycle or trigger unfolds, you will want to go through the process of CBT to heal that response. It would help if you started the process of becoming mindful of the entire thought loop. While you can certainly implement CBT on the fly, it works significantly better if you have a clear picture of what is occurring and how it impacts you.

Each time you go through CBT, you will likely experience faster recovery from former belief systems. However, there may still be specific triggers that are particularly overwhelming and require attention. Even so, you will likely find that even more, intense triggers are easier to overcome because you are more aware of how CBT works, what to expect, and what the process of overcoming unhealthy belief systems looks like.

Chapter Summary

CBT is a psychological practice that is frequently used to change thought patterns, such as those that accompany imposter syndrome. Because it is a complete psychological therapy, it goes significantly more in-depth than affirmations and gratitude journaling. This also means it can have a much substantial impact on helping you recover from imposter syndrome.

To recap, here is what you need to do to employ CBT when overcoming imposter syndrome:

1. Keep a notebook handy and track your thought cycles that lead to imposter syndrome taking root in the first place
2. Identify all the ways that you are attaching your thoughts to false beliefs that are causing you to become emotionally hijacked
3. Create new beliefs you can come back to when imposter syndrome strikes and use them as a part of your inner dialogue to discredit false beliefs
4. If you need to, ask yourself, "Is this really true?" to discredit further false beliefs that may surface
5. Reflect on new opportunities to overcome imposter syndrome with each new trigger you face or thought that surfaces

The more you go through the CBT process the easier it will become as you are familiar with the steps, and how they work. If you face up against a challenging trigger, however, you might find that it requires more effort to stick to your new beliefs and implement them, particularly during an emotional moment of imposter syndrome. Remain consistent and CBT will pay off.

CHAPTER 9

Mindfulness And Healing
Imposter Syndrome

*"Your success will be determined by your own
confidence and fortitude."* – Michelle Obama

Imposter syndrome is a series of thoughts that can rapidly hijack your mind, leaving you feeling as though you are at the mercy of this intrusive thought process. Mindfulness is one excellent way to regain control over your thoughts and gently ease the anxiety of imposter syndrome.

Cultivating mindfulness is a practice that happens over time. Like imposter syndrome has had time to take root, mindfulness needs time to create vital neural pathways in your brain and take root, too. The more you deliberately practice mindfulness, the easier it will be for you to rely on this skill when you need it most. Therefore, you should practice mindfulness even when you feel at peace. This way, when you have imposter syndrome, you can rely on the skills you have been practicing to help you break through and remain calm, balanced, and focused.

The easiest way to cultivate mindfulness is to lean on the seven principles. You can turn them into a practice that can be engaged at any time. The seven principles include non-judgment, patience, curiosity, trust, non-striving, accepting, and releasing.

Principle One: Non-Judgment

Most of us go through our daily lives engaged heavily in the judgment of ourselves, others, and the circumstances and environments we encounter. Learning to embrace non-judgment is a way to refrain from engaging in the psychological biases of your life and enjoy life as it is. This concept might seem strange or even foreign at first, but as you practice it, you will discover how peaceful and enlightening it genuinely is.

It looks something like this: Ryan, my friend from earlier, was judging himself as being an inadequate and unworthy husband. He was afraid of letting down his spouse, so every chance he got, he falsely believed her behavior to be *proof* that he was not measuring up. The more he judged himself, her reactions, and their circumstances, the worse he felt.

By learning to refrain from judgment, Ryan freed up mental space to avoid feeling ashamed, guilty, worthless, and like an imposter. Instead, he opened the opportunity to seek connection, support his wife, and engage positively in fatherhood.

As you go through your daily life, take note of how you judge yourself, others, your circumstances, and your environment. While it is most important to avoid negative judgments, it can also be helpful to cultivate mindfulness around favorable judgments you make as well. While positive judgments can be supportive, they can also reinforce people-pleasing behavior. Ensure that you do not overcorrect imposter syndrome by becoming a people pleaser, which only further supports and internalizes imposter syndrome. Your goal is to seek balance: not to feel guilty about not measuring up and not to feel pressured to prove yourself. When you eliminate both mental processes, you clear space to genuinely engage with life and show up in a meaningful way for yourself and everyone involved.

Principle Two: Patience

Imposter syndrome can bring with it a sense of urgency. As in, you need to relieve your feelings of inadequacy and prove yourself worthy *right now.* This is how Chris, the university student, felt. Despite being a student, he felt pressure to be an expert. He was comparing himself to his father and grandfather, who had significantly more experience than he had. Of course, neither of them was comparing Chris to themselves. They knew he would have to go through the learning process and develop his skills just as they had. Still, the pressure was mounting, and Chris struggled to hold it.

Patience is a crucial mindfulness practice that can help alleviate imposter syndrome by reminding you that *you have time*. You do not have to be *the* expert right away. You also do not have to have everything figured out right away. It is okay and normal to make mistakes. Even the most advanced and experienced make mistakes.

Cultivating patience with yourself, others, life, and the journeys you embrace will help you relieve yourself of the urgency that comes with imposter syndrome. You can develop that patience with affirmations: affirming to yourself that it is safe and suitable to be a beginner, that you have plenty of time to figure things out, and that the learning process is a normal part of the journey. In doing so, you help transition your thoughts from ones that are harming you to ones that are supporting your growth and success.

Principle Three: Curiosity

Alongside a sense of urgency to have it all figured out, imposter syndrome can cause you to feel like you must "know everything" at all times. In reality, those who excel in life do not know everything. Instead, they thrive as experts in their field by acknowledging that they do *not* know everything. They approach every day like it is their first day and through this, embody the beginner's mentality.

This mentality enables them to embrace the learning process and discover all they need to know to continually advance through the various stages of their life journey. Whether it's learning new skills for a job or learning further information to become a better soccer player or parent, they are always in the process of learning.

Embracing the mentality yourself can assist you with becoming more mindful of who you are, where you are in your journey, and how you can embrace *this* moment. A great way to engage with curiosity in each moment is to ask yourself:

1. What do I already know about this situation?
2. Am I sure of that knowledge?
3. What do I *not* know? What information am I lacking?
4. What are ways I could gain that information?
5. How would I approach this if I knew nothing about it?

Often, excellent opportunities to deepen our confidence and buck imposter syndrome are skipped over because we are so focused on "I know." When we shift our focus and embrace learning, we gain new opportunities to discover information that can deepen our skills, build our curiosity, and eliminate the roots of imposter syndrome.

Principle Four: Trust

Trust is a challenging emotion for many. We frequently hear about trust issues people have developed through old relationships or circumstances. Even so, trust is an essential part of developing mindfulness and creating confidence in yourself. This was profound in Alicia's ability to overcome the imposter syndrome she felt when she was promoted to partner at her firm.

Alicia felt she had done an excellent job *selling the image* that she could be a partner. When the partners agreed and invited her to join them, this mindset came back to cause problems. See, Alicia thought she could get herself promoted, but she never considered if she believed she was *capable* of being a partner. Once she was promoted, she questioned whether or not she could fulfill the role she'd been working so hard to receive.

When Alicia began to trust herself to do the same excellent job as partner that she had already been doing as an associate, she felt herself settle into the role. She was no longer concerned with proving herself. Instead, her self-image increased, and she realized she was worthy of the position she'd accepted. The more she sought evidence that this was true, the more she discovered and the deeper she trusted her ability to make good on the promotion she'd earned.

Principle Five: Non-Striving

Striving and imposter syndrome are intimately intertwined. When we have imposter syndrome, we are striving to prove ourselves often by trying to reach goals that we believe will serve as evidence of our worthiness. This can lead to you endlessly pursuing goals and outcomes that you think will help you feel better about your imposter syndrome while simultaneously hiding from others that you are 'incapable.'

Unfortunately, striving to reach these goals will not help you feel better. From this mindset, they reinforce the false belief that you are not capable. What you need to do instead is shift your mindset around your worthiness and abilities and what goals mean to you.

A healthier perspective around your worthiness and abilities can be found by leaning into the other aspects of mindfulness we've already covered: non-judgment, patience, curiosity, and trust. The acceptance we will discuss in the next section is supportive of this, also. For goals, a healthier perspective is to view them as an opportunity to see what you are capable of rather than an opportunity to prove you are worthy of what you have. When goals are used to encourage yourself to expand beyond your comfort zone to experience more passion, joy, and pleasure in life, they are being appropriately used as tools to better your existence.

To shift the goals you presently have, ask yourself: why am I pursuing this? What will I gain from the outcome? If your answers align with 'someone else's approval' or 'feeling worthy,' discard those goals immediately. Instead, pursue the ones that align with solutions like 'to experience being better at ___' or 'to discover my potential.' In following the latter goals, you stop striving and begin expanding into your desired life. Through this, you thoroughly enjoy the present and the future, which is a significantly healthier experience of life than that afforded through imposter syndrome, striving, and proving yourself.

Principle Six: Accepting

If you struggle with imposter syndrome, I can almost guarantee you also struggle with accepting yourself and life as it is. In addition to feeling incompetent or like you are playing a charade for others, you also likely feel as though the 'real you' incapable, unworthy, and unacceptable. You may spend much of your life fighting who you are, how you are, and what you are.

While a certain degree of discomfort is excellent for encouraging you grow beyond where you have presently grown to, approaching life with a complete lack of acceptance of yourself and your circumstances is unhealthy. It leads to a low self-image and self-esteem, which serves as a breeding ground for experiences such as imposter syndrome.

Learning to take yourself as you are is essential, as is learning to accept circumstances. In doing so, you relieve yourself of the feeling of being a victim or a fraud and immediately give yourself full permission to be who you are here and now. You accept yourself *with* feelings of inadequacy and worthlessness, not despite them. You accept the circumstances of your life. You accept the personality traits you do, and do not like about yourself. Ultimately, you lean into complete acceptance of everything, including yourself, as it is.

In doing so, you release the urgent need to "fix" anything, because nothing needs to be fixed. Instead, everything is simply growing along a natural path of life, and you can enjoy the different phases as they come. Even the less pleasant ones are more enjoyable when you lean into acceptance because you understand that they are essential to the journey and that they will not last forever.

Principle Seven: Releasing

Acceptance becomes the perfect segue for releasing, which is the final principle of mindfulness that will serve you in releasing your imposter syndrome. If you are encouraged to accept everything as it is, including yourself, then that means you must also release everything associated with non-acceptance.

For example, Alicia had to release her feeling of being inadequate and unworthy of being a partner, even though that was a real thought and emotional experience she was having. She had to accept that this was now her role and that she had earned it and therefore she had two options: to accept it and fulfill it (and therefore release feelings of inadequacy) or to walk away from it. Of course, she chose to accept it and release ill thoughts and feelings that were holding her back.

Chris had to release the feeling of being inadequate and unworthy alongside his father and grandfather. Even though he had these thoughts and feelings and they felt real to him, he had to either accept that they were not ultimately true and choose to put the work in to become an excellent investment banker or walk away from the family legacy. He chose to accept himself, complete with his knowledge and abilities, and trust that he would one day be as great as his father and grandfather were.

Ryan had to release the feelings of being inadequate and unworthy as a husband and father. Even though he thought and felt this way, he needed to accept that he was capable of being both an excellent husband and father and choose to act accordingly. In doing so, he had to release his fears and the limiting beliefs that held him back and walk boldly into this reality. As a result, his marriage began to thrive, and he began to genuinely enjoy fatherhood.

You, too, have a choice. You can accept that your imposter syndrome is ultimately untrue and choose to release it and take the steps to grow from where you are, or you can walk away from everything you have created. One thing is for certain, however. You cannot remain where you are, allowing imposter syndrome to take over continually. You must heal it and be done with it for good by deliberately accepting that it happens, trusting that it is not ultimately true, and releasing it each time it surfaces. If you don't, it is only a matter of time before your self-sabotage again and destroy everything you have worked so hard to create.

A Daily Mindfulness Practice

Having a specific, step by step daily mindfulness practice is a great way to support yourself with leaning into mindfulness and making use of it on a regular basis. The easiest daily mindfulness routine comes in two steps: the first is a journaling practice you can do each morning and night. The second step is to practice "mindful minutes" Throughout your day.

In your mindfulness journal each morning and night, answer the following:

1. Who am I judging right now, for what, and why? What do I gain from this? Are my judgments ultimately true?

2. What am I trying to rush in life right now? Why? How am I hurting myself by attempting to rush the process? How can I slow down and take a more balanced approach?

3. Where am I allowing myself to be a know-it-all? In what ways am I possibly cutting corners or missing opportunities by acting like I know it all? How can I apply a curiosity-based mindset to this area of my life?

4. Where am I not trusting myself? Why? How can I trust myself more?

5. In what ways am I striving right now? What am I striving for? Will it really give me the outcome I desire? What could I do instead?

6. Am I truly accepting myself as I am right now? Am I accepting my life as it is right now? Where can I be more accepting of myself and my circumstances?

7. What am I holding onto that is holding me back? How can I let it go? What would this area of my life look like without the resistance?

In addition to this journaling practice you can establish a mindful minute practice. For your mindful minute you will block out 60-seconds, close your eyes, and focus on the next three breaths. Then, you will check-in with your thoughts. Once you clearly see what your thought process looks like, ask yourself: is this ultimately true? Is this helpful or hurtful to what I desire from life? What is a better thought to have right now? Once you have discovered the better thought you can open your eyes and re-engage with the room around you.

As you do, use the better thought as an affirmation and anchor it into the present moment by saying "right now in ___ I am ___ and I will now ___." For example, "right now in my office I am fully capable of being an excellent employee and I will now do the paperwork that needs to get done" or "right now in my home I am fully capable of being an excellent mother and I will now prepare snacks so we can have a games night together." In doing this, you anchor your mindfulness into the present space and change the trajectory of your thoughts and feelings in this moment, which is the only moment you can truly impact from this space anyway.

Chapter Summary

Mindfulness is a powerful way to anchor your mind into the present moment and align it with truth. This practice is not specific to imposter syndrome, but it does have a significant impact on healing imposter syndrome.

Through this chapter you have discovered:

- The seven principles of mindfulness (non-judgment, patience, curiosity, trust, non-striving, accepting, and releasing.)
- How to apply these seven principles to imposter syndrome
- A daily mindfulness journaling practice that will help you take control over your thoughts
- A daily mindful minute practice to anchor you into the present moment as needed

These skills are imperative to rapidly eliminating imposter syndrome in the moment and anchoring yourself into a new reality by deliberately changing your thoughts and subsequent emotions! You should practice them daily, even when you are not actively experiencing imposter syndrome, so they are stronger and more supportive when you are.

CHAPTER 10

Positive Coping Mechanisms
And Imposter Syndrome

"One of the greatest discoveries a man makes, one of his greatest surprises, is to find he can do what he was afraid he couldn't do." – Henry Ford

Although coping mechanisms are frequently referred to as a negative thing, plenty of positive coping mechanisms exist, too. While we may all agree that chewing your nails when you are anxious is not ideal, we can also likely agree that focusing on your breath when you are anxious is a great approach to dealing with that often intense emotion. It may surprise you to know that *both* of these responses are coping mechanisms, though one of them is clearly preferred to the other.

Cultivating your own positive coping mechanisms with imposter syndrome is an excellent way to overcome it. While it may not eliminate the troubling syndrome at its roots, it will still allow you to take back control over your mind and move in a positive direction whenever the intrusive thoughts occur. An ounce of prevention may be worth a pound of cure, but I think anyone struggling with something undesirable can agree that relief from the symptoms itself is just as desirable.

In this chapter, we will cover key coping mechanisms that can help you identify and eradicate the symptoms of imposter syndrome as they surface. This way, you can rapidly take back control and navigate any situation with ease, even those which may have once been impossible to navigate.

Seek Out A Skilled Mentor

No matter which area of your life you are experiencing imposter syndrome with, I can guarantee someone else has experienced it, too. Even areas where it seems like imposter syndrome doesn't "make sense" can be plagued by these thoughts. Take Eric, for example. Eric was a few pounds overweight and struggling to get to a size he felt good about. Despite knowing how important exercise was to his success, he struggled to consistently show up. He did everything he was supposed to: he scheduled times for exercise, purchased a gym membership, packed his gym bag, and prepared healthy meals. Still, he couldn't get himself to take the commitment seriously.

Why not? Because Eric felt imposter syndrome every time he showed up for a workout. Even working out at home seemed impossible because he felt so insecure about himself that the idea of exercising *period* felt uncomfortable.

Upon hiring a personal trainer who was familiar with this mindset, Eric discovered that this type of imposter syndrome is completely normal. Many people experience it in many areas of their lives. By hiring a mentor who understood this unique experience, Eric tapped into the potential of having a skilled peer who could coach him through the challenging thoughts and find confidence in his exercise routine. Within a couple weeks, Eric felt confident at the gym. Within a couple months, he loved showing up for his workouts. By the six month mark Eric lost the extra weight and turned his focus to toning his body and expanding his strength and stamina. All because he was brave enough to acknowledge that his thoughts were holding him back and that, through receiving help, he could overcome these challenges and reach his goal.

By seeking out your own mentor, you, too, can receive guided assistance through all the challenging thoughts and experiences you have. Plus, you have the confidence of knowing that anything you might get stuck on can be sorted out with the support of another individual who may have more experience or insight than you. Through this, you develop your confidence, and your imposter syndrome naturally fades.

The positive coping mechanism: find *and actively communicate with* a mentor.

Focus On The Facts

Imposter syndrome thrives on your emotions – not solid facts. The more you *feel* like an imposter, the worse it gets. This compounding fear accelerates regardless of what the facts are. An excellent way to stop imposter syndrome in its tracks is to focus on the facts. Often, the facts support a different reality than the ones your emotions are feeding into. By focusing on them you can defeat the falsehoods of your emotions and experience relief from your imposter syndrome symptoms.

An excellent way to get beyond the emotional side of imposter syndrome and lean into the facts is to ask yourself questions like:

1. What, specifically, am I feeling right now?
2. Are these feelings based on fact or fiction?
3. What reality do they support?
4. What reality would I like to be experiencing?
5. What facts back that reality up?
6. Is there any action I need to take *right now* to create the reality I desire?

Occasionally, your fears may be founded. For example, you might be stuck on a project at work because you do not have all the information you need. In that case, you are not dealing with imposter syndrome, you are dealing with a genuine lack of information.

You may, however, feel that your imposter syndrome is triggered when you consider asking someone for that information because you do not want to be perceived as incapable or unknowledgeable. In that case, you can again go through the questions. You will likely discover in that round of the questioning process that asking questions is not indicative of you being an incapable worker. Rather, this means you are a skilled worker with a meticulous eye for detail. This is an admirable quality to have and is one you can feel proud about. If you focus on this truth: that it is admirable to have a meticulous eye for detail in your line of work, then your imposter syndrome no longer has a reason to take hold. It is unfounded and, therefore, perfunctory.

The positive coping mechanism: focus on the facts more than you focus on your fears.

Learn To Be Proud Of Yourself

If there's one thing we've touched on frequently throughout this book, it's that imposter syndrome has a way of making you feel less than. Allowing yourself to remain in this mental space for long periods can lead to you genuinely believing you are unworthy of celebration or praise. Fortunately, this is not true. As you focus on the facts, you will also discover that there is plenty of *good* about you.

Focusing on the good about you gives you the opportunity to see how incredible you are, and how much you have contributed to the world around you. If you allow yourself to, you can even find several reasons to be proud of yourself. This might seem like a stretch when you are dealing with imposter syndrome, but it is something you can learn to think about and feel.

Becoming proud of yourself begins by choosing to think thoughts that align with pride. For example:

- "I may have felt worried about work, but I showed up and did an incredible job on that report today."
- "I may have felt unworthy in my marriage, but I still took the time to connect with my spouse today and that felt wonderful."
- "I may have felt anxious about my studies, but I still showed up and scored an amazing grade on that test."
- "I may have felt uncomfortable going to the gym, but I showed up and worked out and left feeling great about myself."

Understand that creating pride isn't about declaring that you approached a situation perfectly. Certainly, you can still feel anxious, fearful, uncomfortable, overwhelmed, unworthy, or any other number of emotions. The point is not that you felt these feelings, it's that you found a way to take a positive step in spite of feeling them. Celebrating yourself for these things and cultivating a sense of pride expands your confidence and enables you to grow past imposter syndrome.

Another way to be proud of yourself is to genuinely invest in your skills. When you invest in yourself and set a standard for how you do things, you create a clear guideline against which you can measure your work. So long as your standards are realistic and reasonable, this can support you with knowing that you've done a great job and you can feel proud of the effort you've put in.

The positive coping mechanism: learn to internalize feelings of pride in yourself and your work.

Confide In Someone You Trust

Active imposter syndrome can feel incredibly isolating. You might feel like you have to hide your feelings of inadequacy because if you don't someone will 'find you out' and everything you have will be lost. Unfortunately, all too many people submit to this fear by remaining in this isolated state and fail to ever vocalize what they are experiencing. As a result, their imposter syndrome gets worse.

By sharing how you feel, you create the opportunity to expand beyond the isolation and limitation of imposter syndrome and experience relief from your symptoms. This happens on two levels: first, by expressing and therefore releasing your emotions. Second, by potentially finding others who have experienced the same feelings and who can provide empathy and guidance on how to move beyond your symptoms.

When you actively express your emotions, they move through your body. You gain the opportunity to work through the thoughts, feelings, and experiences that come with them. This is preferable to holding them in, hiding them, and having your feelings grow worse while also being shrouded by shame and fear. It is a good idea to find someone, or a few people, you can confide in who will reliably meet you with empathy and compassion in your emotions. In doing so, you feel safe expressing your feelings relating to imposter syndrome and can work through them and release them as often as you need to. If you find that you are venting 'too much,' hiring a therapist is a great alternative to confiding in friends. Therapists can be invaluable in listening, empathizing, and offering guidance of what to do next.

The positive coping mechanism: find someone to confide in and express your thoughts and feelings about imposter syndrome.

Acknowledge And Validate Your Feelings

This particular coping mechanism was best learned by Ryan, the gentleman who experienced imposter syndrome in his marriage from chapter 1. See, Ryan admitted some of his feelings to his wife periodically throughout their marriage. Still, he continued to feel unworthy and incapable of being the husband and father he was supposed to be. Regardless of how she reassured him, he never felt better. Instead, he felt as though she was just being nice to him. This made him feel worse because, in addition to feeling self-conscious, he also felt like a burden that required excessive validation from his wife who was already busy with their newborn.

To get beyond imposter syndrome, Ryan didn't need validation from his wife. Instead, he needed to acknowledge and validate himself. As he learned how to acknowledge that he felt fearful and unworthy, he also learned how to validate that this was normal and okay. Finding this validation and acceptance within himself enabled him to stop feeling like an emotional burden to his wife *and* helped him grow beyond the fear and doubts he was experiencing. Because he was no longer wrestling with so many different emotions that blocked him from expressing himself in his marriage and fatherhood, Ryan became the husband and father he always wanted to be.

In your life, this might look like acknowledging that you are feeling doubtful, unworthy, incapable, or fearful of the role you have taken on. Then, with that acknowledgment in mind, you can seek to validate yourself and the emotions you are experiencing. It is likely that your feelings are entirely normal and have been felt by many in your situation. By recognizing this, you realize that what you feel is not unique or unusual but perfectly reasonable. You can also acknowledge that, despite these feelings, they are not ultimately true, and there are facts you can focus on that help you move beyond the emotions and grow beyond imposter syndrome.

The positive coping mechanism: acknowledge and validate your feelings to avoid feeling ashamed of your thoughts and emotions.

Look For The Evidence

Because imposter syndrome relies heavily on how we *feel* rather than what is *true*, looking for evidence is one of the most potent positive coping mechanisms you can depend on. We have touched on it plenty in this book, so rather than repeating what I have already explained, I want to focus instead on what you can do to turn this into a positive coping mechanism.

Turning "looking for evidence" into a positive coping mechanism requires you to cultivate a certain level of self-awareness around what your current thought processes are in each moment. Your mindfulness routine will be incredibly beneficial for your ability to recognize the moment you begin experiencing thoughts associated with imposter syndrome. Identifying these thoughts as close to the beginning ensures they do not gain momentum. This way, you do not get carried away with the thoughts and feelings that come with imposter syndrome.

Understand that it is natural for you to get swept up with the momentum and carried away with the emotions when you first begin this process. Even if you are aware of the imposter syndrome, you may find that it is still challenging to break the momentum at first. This is because you are so used to this reaction to circumstances that trigger it that it has become a well-established habit. Not to fear. You can break it.

The best way to break this habit is to immediately seek proof that disproves the imposter syndrome. Look for evidence that you are good, capable, and worthy. Avoid looking for evidence that would make you feel *more* like an imposter. For example, rather than saying, "I'm just a student," say, "I'm doing a fantastic job at learning! I'm a capable learner. Here's why ___." This shift in your approach will immediately begin to break the cycle of imposter syndrome and inspire feelings of confidence, courage, and capability.

The positive coping mechanism: look for evidence that you are capable.

Reframe Your Thoughts With Mindfulness

Looking for evidence the moment you experience imposter syndrome is an excellent way to stop these thoughts in their track. Another ideal approach is to reframe your thoughts with mindfulness. While looking for evidence enables you to look to the 'contrary,' reframing your thoughts with mindfulness helps you accept where you are and move on regardless.

Eric provided an excellent example of how this looks in action. When Eric was at the beginning of his weight loss journey, he did everything he could to feel better about himself. Still, no matter how he looked at it, he was overweight and lacked the motivation to work out when feeling so much imposter syndrome at the gym. Rather than lying to himself about how he was feeling or reaching for evidence to make himself feel better, Eric accepted how he was feeling and acknowledged that the only way he would ever feel better was by taking meaningful action toward a resolution. So, he hired a personal trainer to mentor him.

As you know, acknowledging and validating your feelings is a powerful way to shift them. You can then lean into the process of mindfully understanding that progress will require you to act regardless of how you feel in the moment. For example, if you feel afraid or doubtful of your ability, you must try anyway. As you cultivate this mindfulness and deliberately take action from your present state, you begin to create a more desirable outcome. As a result, you begin to curate the evidence you need to change your mindset even sooner.

The positive coping mechanism: reframe your thoughts with mindfulness.

Anticipate The Symptoms

Finally, another excellent way to cope with imposter syndrome is to anticipate it. If you regularly experience imposter syndrome, chances are you know precisely what circumstances are likely to trigger it. Predicting your symptoms not only allows you to prepare for them in advance, but also reduces the impact they have because you know they will happen *and* that they are not inherently true.

This proactive awareness "sucks the wind from its sails," so to speak, by disempowering the ideas associated with imposter syndrome. For many, when they can anticipate it is coming, the thoughts themselves have a 'fake' or 'untrue' feeling associated with them. This prevents their ability to gain momentum and take root and leaves you feeling more empowered to choose different thoughts and experience a different outcome at the moment.

A significant key to consider is that anticipating imposter syndrome *as it is,* may make you feel worse. You must expect it *while also recognizing it as being false and curable.* An excellent way to do this is to anticipate that you will respond in a more healthily and stably manner when it strikes next. For example, rather than believing it, you will acknowledge it for what it is and choose to believe that you are capable and worthy. By taking this approach, your anticipation becomes a superpower instead of a self-sabotage.

The positive coping mechanism: anticipate imposter syndrome and disempower it in advance.

Chapter Summary

Sometimes, imposter syndrome cannot be prevented entirely. Instead, the best thing you can do is lean into positive coping tools that help you stop it from gaining momentum when it strikes. Positive coping mechanisms work best when practiced repeatedly, so you develop habits around them, similarly to how you have cultivated habits that reinforce imposter syndrome.

The eight best positive coping mechanisms for imposter syndrome are:

- Seeking out a skilled mentor
- Focusing on the facts
- Learning to be proud of yourself
- Confiding in someone you trust
- Acknowledging and validating your feelings
- Looking for evidence
- Reframing your thoughts with mindfulness
- Anticipating the symptoms

Ideally, you should turn to these positive coping mechanisms as soon as you recognize you are dealing with imposter syndrome. This way, you can rapidly shift your thoughts, and, therefore, your feelings. With enough practice, these new positive coping mechanisms will become your habitual response to imposter syndrome and the symptoms of your syndrome will no longer concern you.

PART THREE

BODY LANGUAGE
AND CONFIDENCE

CHAPTER 11

Body Language And Confidence

"Confidence is the most beautiful thing you can possess." – Sabrina Carpenter

B ody language is one of the most essential elements of communication. This non-verbal communication style supports us in relaying and decoding messages to and from each other. A person's body language can change a statement's context based on their emotional state. For example, "What are you doing?" combined with a slight head tilt implies curiosity, while "What are you doing?" combined with crossed arms indicates irritation or anger.

We first became aware of the importance of body language in the early 1950s when anthropologist Ray Birdwhistell took an interest in non-verbal communication methods. Later, in 1969, we discovered a phenomenon termed 'biofeedback.' Biofeedback is the process of your thoughts being influenced by your physical reality. For example, if you are cold, your body sends a message to your brain about your temperature, and your brain formulates thoughts about getting warm.

What does this have to do with imposter syndrome? A lot, actually.

How You Carry Yourself Affects How You Perceive Yourself

Thanks to biofeedback, how you carry yourself doesn't just communicate who you are or what you think to other people. It also expresses who you are and how you feel about *yourself.* Learning to carry yourself in a way that conveys confidence, ability, and self-worth is a powerful way to leverage biofeedback and train your brain to see yourself as a confident and capable person.

There are several little things you can do to boost your self-confidence with body language. I suggest beginning by implementing one or two at a time. Then, as they become more comfortable, you can start to implement more. This is what Alicia did when she was developing self-confidence when she first started as an associate at the firm where she is now a partner. Taking her time helped her naturalize different types of body language and become used to that level of language. It also ensured that the people around her didn't feel like she had changed too much at once. Instead, they noticed a gradual yet powerful increase in her self-confidence over time. One which may have led to the confidence that ultimately earned her a position as a partner at her firm.

12 Body Languages That Inspire Self-Confidence

There are numerous movements in body language that communicate virtually every emotion you can experience. Chances are, your present body language expresses fear, discomfort, and inferiority to yourself. This further reinforces the feelings of imposter syndrome as they come up. While there are many different body languages you can lean into that will help communicate confidence, these twelve are the best.

Make Eye Contact

Eye contact is a powerful means of communicating confidence. Ideally, you want to make eye contact for about 60% of a conversation, so make eye contact for a few moments then break eye contact and look elsewhere.

Slow Your Movements

Moving quickly makes you appear more anxious, and it can make you feel more anxious, too. Slower, more intentional movements are ideal for helping you feel calmer and communicate a more peaceful presence to those around you.

Keep Your Chin Up

Whether you're walking somewhere or talking to someone, make a point to keep your chin up and face straight ahead. Look directly at where you are going or who you are talking to. Angle your chin slightly up. This pose boosts confidence and makes you look like a more decisive leader as well.

Take Larger Steps

Short, quick steps are indicative of nervousness and rapid movements. Taking slower, longer steps is a great way to help communicate confidence and authority. If you are wearing high heels, walk slower and take the most prominent step you comfortably gain without losing balance. The more you practice, the easier it becomes.

Lean Forward

Where your body is leaning toward indicates interest, confidence, and certainty. In conversations with others, aim to lean slightly toward them as you talk. Leaning in shows you are engaged in the conversation and comfortable in their presence.

Watch Your Hands

Where you place your hands says a lot about how you feel. Touching your face or neck is an excellent way to communicate nervousness. Instead, try positioning your hands like a steeple or holding them palm up in your lap. These better communicate confidence.

Don't Fidget

Fidgeting is a sure sign of fear, anxiety, and discomfort. It communicates to others, as well as to yourself that you are out of your element and trying to soothe yourself. Practice keeping yourself still and in a comfortable position that you can maintain. If you tend to fidget with the stuff in your hands or nearby, make a point of putting things down or sitting slightly away from things you habitually fiddle with.

Give Firm Handshakes

Firm handshakes are an excellent sign of confidence. They communicate to others that you view yourself as an authority figure, and they communicate to yourself that you see yourself as worthy of strength and confidence. If you are uncomfortable with handshakes, practice with a loved one or a coworker willing to give you feedback and guide you toward a more substantial, firmer handshake.

Stand Up Straight

When you feel fearful or uncomfortable, it can be easy to slouch. Make a point to straighten your spine, drop your shoulders back and away from your ears, and uncross your arms and legs. An open posture communicates confidence, self-assurance, and leadership.

Mirror Body Language

When you are communicating with someone, mirroring body language is an excellent sign that you are engaged and interested in what they are saying. This behavior also communicates to yourself that you see yourself as their equal. Mainly when you communicate with people you admire and respect, this is an excellent way to boost how you admire and respect yourself, too.

Avoid Using Pockets

Like fidgeting makes you look fearful, uncertain, and unconfident, keeping your hands in your pockets can do the same. Keep your hands out of your pockets. Holding them on your lap or the arms of the chair you are sitting in is a better position for your hands when talking.

Speak Slowly And Clearly

Lastly, rushing your words is a sure way to feel anxious and communicate fear. Plus, if someone must ask for clarification because you have spoken too fast, that can lead to further nervousness. Instead, slow down, speak clearly, and give yourself time to say everything you need to say. In doing so, you command respect and communicate confidence while also boosting your self-confidence.

Chapter Summary

Body language is a powerful means of communicating confidence to others. It is also an excellent way to convey trust in yourself through biofeedback. There are many body language styles you can learn, but the twelve indicated are best for helping boost self-confidence. You should only shift one or two at a time to avoid paying excessive attention to your body language and feeling uncomfortable and unnatural in different situations. Once you feel comfortable with a specific type of body language, you can move on to the next one. Over time, you will have assimilated all twelve types of body language and will be regularly communicating confidence to yourself and those around you!

CHAPTER 12

Body Language For
Confidence In Social Settings

"All you need in life is ignorance and confidence,
and then success is sure." – Mark Twain

The twelve signs of body language I shared in the previous chapter are excellent for communicating confidence to *yourself.* While they will all communicate confidence to those around you, as well, the goal was to heighten how you feel about yourself, so you command your presence with greater certainty.

In addition to these twelve steps, there are additional steps you can take to communicate confidence in social settings. The following six steps will help you take your body language further and communicate confidence to those around you. In doing so, you build a positive rapport with them. The more others view you in high esteem, the more likely you may be to view yourself in high regard, particularly if you combine this with evidence of your worth and ability.

Plant Your Feet With An Open And Wide Stance

Keeping your legs crossed or pointed the opposite direction of who you are speaking with communicates that you are closed off and unreceptive to the conversation. Even if your words express otherwise, your body language communicates that you are disengaged and unwilling to genuinely interact with the other person.

A better way to communicate confidence is to open your feet. If you are a lady, it is generally accepted to keep your knees together and your feet closer together. However, you still want to keep your feet slightly separated and point directly toward the person you are speaking with. If you are a man, your knees can be separated, and you can have your feet wider apart.

When standing, keeping your feet about hip-width apart or slightly wider and your feet firmly planted on the floor communicates confidence. Do not lift your feet, bounce on them, sway back and forth, or otherwise lean into a fluid posture. Instead, stand firm, commanding your presence on a solid foundation.

Use Your Head To Communicate Agreement

It can be unsettling to communicate with someone staring directly at you while you speak yet who remains perfectly still. We are used to the person we are sharing with moving around, and while excessive or erratic movements indicate nervousness, some degree of movement is expected.

An appropriate way to move your body when listening to someone else speak is to use your head. Nodding in agreement or disagreement shows that you are listening and engaged. You can also use facial expressions to communicate that you are listening. Raising your eyebrows in surprise, narrowing them to express your focus, and keeping them soft to express neutrality or empathy, for example, are all excellent ways to communicate when you are the listener.

The key to using nods and facial expressions to communicate confidence and bypass imposter syndrome is to use expressions that are natural for you. If you are not generally a high-energy person, exaggerated nods or highly expressive facial movements will seem unnatural. They will feel bizarre and, worse, uncomfortable for the other person, too. Instead, you want to take your time and express yourself in a way that is natural for your energy level.

Open Your Body To The Person In Front Of You

You can reveal a lot about who you are, how you think, what you feel, your attitude toward life, and your confidence in yourself by how you hold your body when you share with other people. There are two different types of postures you might use: open and closed. Both can communicate confidence in different circumstances, though you are more likely to use a relaxed stance in social events. Closed postures convey confidence when you have asserted a firm boundary or decision and are showcasing that you are not available for further discussion or negotiation.

Opening your body posture means sitting with your knees uncrossed, your arms uncrossed, your hands open and palm up or relaxed in your lap, and your shoulders square and facing the person in front of you. You should be looking directly at them, as well, keeping your chin up and eyes on them. An open body posture achieves two things: it shows that you are comfortable and confident in the present circumstance, and it allows the person you're speaking with to feel the same. As that energy is reciprocated, you will begin to feel a genuine sense of comfort and confidence wash over you and the interaction will feel more natural and less calculated.

Remove Any Barriers Between You And Them

Body language is primarily determined by, as you likely guessed, your *body.* However, it is not just about how you move and use your body when communicating that portrays confidence and certainty around others. Where you place your body and how expresses confidence as well. People who sit down behind desks or with some form of a physical barrier between them and others in the room unconsciously show that they are uncomfortable, unconfident, or trying to protect themselves.

In some circumstances, such as if you invite people to your office for a meeting, it is natural that there will be a desk between you and the people you are talking to. In these cases, your position can assert authority. In most circumstances, however, you want to avoid putting anything between you and the people you are with. Choose a seat that is not blocked off from the rest of the room, do not hold a purse or briefcase or any belonging on your lap that would block you off from others, and keep your body facing the people you are communicating with.

An excellent stereotype comes to mind to portray the reasoning behind this form of body language. A girl I knew named Erica used to do this. The stereotype is an intern or a new employee in a high-powered corporate office standing shyly in the corner of the room clutching files or a briefcase to their chest. It may seem harmless, but the image communicates one of low self-confidence and low self-assurance in their environment. As I told Erica: you need to remove all barriers between you and the room around you, command your space, and show up like you own the place. It takes confidence, but it will transform the way you feel, and the way people respond to you.

Smile A Lot More Than You Think You Should

Another thing I taught Erica was to smile. I don't mean a fake smile or an exaggerated one, either. A simple upturn of your lips is a beautiful way to soften your appearance, give yourself a friendlier expression, and communicate confidence. Especially in corporate situations, it can feel like smiling too much might make you look like a "brown noser." You want people to think of you as serious and confident. The thing is: confidence isn't always about being serious. It's about knowing how to read the room and engage accordingly and being secure enough in yourself that you can show up happy with who you are and what you bring to the table.

When you have imposter syndrome, feeling sure of yourself and confident in what you bring to the table might feel impossible. You can begin to lean into what it would feel like, though, by smiling and engaging positively with the people around you.

Do Not Change Your Posture Too Often

Lastly, it is important not to change your posture too often. When you do, you communicate that you are uncomfortable. Occasionally moving suggests genuine physical discomfort but moving too frequently may indicate that you are uncomfortable with the situation and that you are having a difficult time managing your nerves. Practice finding a couple of positions you feel comfortable in and maintain those.

If it is true that your nerves are getting the best of you and you are moving because of them, try soothing yourself with something simple like a sip of water or an activity you might perform that is relevant to the circumstances. For example, if you are in a meeting, you might take notes, or at home with your partner, you might get something for them or do something nice to serve them. Getting out of stagnancy and into positive motion is an excellent way to comfort yourself while building your confidence in social circumstances.

Chapter Summary

Body language can extend beyond communicating confidence to yourself and into communicating confidence to those around you. This form of body language helps you get beyond imposter syndrome by supporting you with feeling confident around your peers. As you feel confident around them, this, combined with their confidence in you, boosts your self-image. Naturally, your imposter syndrome will begin to fade, and you will feel more secure in who you are. The more you embrace this communication style, the better you will feel.

PART FOUR

EXERCISES FOR OVERCOMING
IMPOSTER SYNDROME

CHAPTER 13

Exercises That Help Overcome Imposter Syndrome

"It's not what you are that holds you back, it's what you think you are not." – Denis Waitley

P lenty of the work you do to overcome imposter syndrome will be repetitive work that takes place over several practice runs. Each time imposter syndrome strikes, you will implement these practices and help lessen the blow. Gradually, the symptoms reduce, and eventually, they disappear altogether. On the odd occasion when they rear their head, and it's easy to see them for what they are and release them. If they do happen to spiral again, you can take control and eliminate them more quickly because you have the skills to do so.

While these practices are an excellent way to eliminate imposter syndrome, there are additional ways you can overcome imposter syndrome by facilitating breakthroughs with specific exercises to help you see things differently. These break-throughs are designed to help you deeply assess the experiences causing imposter syndrome in the first place and eliminate them from the root cause.

The seven exercises we go through in this section of the book will help you eliminate imposter syndrome, so you never have to deal with it again.

I have briefly described each one below so you can determine which breakthrough would be most helpful to you with the im-poster syndrome you are experiencing.

Changing Your Narrative

If you've been paying attention, one of the biggest things con-tributing to imposter syndrome is your thoughts. The way you think about yourself affects the way you feel about yourself. While we have done a significant amount of work around what you tell yourself throughout the day, there is a deeper layer we can tap into: your inner narrative about who you are, what you are capable of, and how successful you can be at it. In this exer-cise, we will completely transform the way you see yourself and the story you tell yourself daily, so imposter syndrome doesn't stand a chance.

Regulating Your Emotions

Because imposter syndrome is so closely linked with your thoughts and emotions, deliberate emotional regulation skills are powerful for assisting you with overcoming the emotional dysregulation that surfaces during bouts of imposter syndrome. These skills will also help you overcome anxiety and other forms of fear that may sabotage you from experiencing setbacks.

Building Your Self-Control And Self-Discipline

All forms of fear, including imposter syndrome, bring an intense emotional spiral. As you will learn during the emotional regulation practices, this can lead to emotional hijacking and dysregulation. In addition to building skills in regulating your emotions, you can build skills in self-control and self-discipline. These skills will deepen your self-trust and assist you with feeling confident in overcoming anything in life.

Becoming Your Most Compassionate Supporter

It is sometimes true that people who experience imposter syndrome has experienced significant pressure from others to act in a way that is not in alignment with who they are. For example, a parent might have pressured you to pursue a skill or career that you were not interested in or ridiculed you for the path you were interested in. By becoming your most compassionate supporter you give yourself permission to step beyond their harsh criticisms and embrace a life you truly desire – complete with your own cheerleading and support.

Embracing Your Innate Strengths

Imposter syndrome can routinely lead to you focusing on your weaknesses instead of your strengths. When you learn to focus on and enhance your strengths, imposter syndrome no longer feels as intimidating because you realize that there are things you are genuinely great at. Although it is true that you will indeed have weaknesses, too, knowing you are excellent at specific skills allows you to leverage those skills and boost your ability to feel good about yourself and what you bring to the table.

Healing Perfectionism

Some people pick up the false belief that they must be perfect at what they do to be considered successful. This can stem from childhood or a variety of different experiences throughout adulthood. For some people, it appears to be a personality trait they were born with. Regardless of where it comes from, perfectionism can enhance imposter syndrome by stimulating the narrative that you are never good enough. Overcoming perfectionism, then, is a great way to grow beyond imposter syndrome and find confidence in yourself.

Chapter Summary

Continued practices help overcome the habit of imposter syndrome, but sometimes imposter syndrome can be healed with
meaningful breakthroughs. These breakthroughs can rapidly
change your perception of yourself or your circumstances, effectively disintegrating the roots of imposter syndrome. In the
coming chapters, we will discuss in-depth strategies to facilitate
these breakthroughs in your life. You can begin with the ones
that make the most sense to you and your experience with imposter syndrome.

CHAPTER 14

Changing Your Narrative

"What you think about yourself is much more
important than what others think of you."
— Seneca the Elder

What you tell yourself matters. By now, you understand this to be true. You have seen how, in each
story I've shared with you throughout this book,
the person's reality was heavily impacted their thoughts. Even
when their thoughts weren't true, their reality was affected as
though they were. This is why we have done extensive work to
shift your ideas *at the moment.*

But what if you could shift your thoughts sooner than that?

What if, instead of convincing herself she was worthy, Alicia
went into the next level of her career, already knowing she was?
What if, instead of convincing himself he was capable of being
a good husband and dad, Ryan already believed he was? What

if, instead of thinking he had to prove himself to be worthy, Chris already thought he was?

What if, instead of convincing yourself that you are worthy or capable, you already believed and knew you were?

This is the change that comes with changing your narrative.

Your Sense Of Identity Defines Your Personality

Many believe that thoughts, emotions, and actions are the core drivers of change. For this entire book, we have described different ways to transform your thoughts, emotions, and actions. While these are all powerful tools for eliminating imposter syndrome, there is a deeper layer you can connect with that will transform your life entirely. That is: changing how you identify yourself.

At the core of everything you do is your identity. This is not about how others identify you but how you identify yourself. When you think about who you are at the core of your being, how do you describe yourself? Do you think you are inherently good or bad? Do you believe you are worthy? Capable? Significant? Meaningful? A good friend? A strong team player? Excellent at your career?

Those struggling with imposter syndrome generally believe that, at their core, they are *not* the person they have been living as. For example, Alicia thought she was playing the role of a partner at the law firm, but this was not a part of her core identity. Instead, she saw herself as good at climbing the ladder of success, but not necessarily someone who was capable of fulfilling the varying roles she embraced. She had to change her core identity to discover that she was, in fact, an incredible lawyer and undoubtedly worthy of the role she had landed.

How Do You Identify Yourself?

Discovering your own identity, according to you, is an excellent opportunity to understand where you are enabling imposter syndrome and other similar thought processes to take root. The troubling part of this process is that you will likely discover that much of your present identity has been determined by other people. Often, that is why imposter syndrome takes over.

Your mom said to you that you were too loud when you spoke. Your dad said to you that you were too weak because you couldn't score a goal in soccer. Your sister said to you that you were a jerk because you broke her toy when you were kids. Your best friend told you that you were a horrible friend because you accidentally hurt their feelings. For some reason, all these remarks became a piece of how you identify yourself, and now you are afraid people will "figure you out."

In reality, it is *you* who needs to figure you out. Chances are, you are none of the horrible things you fear you are. Instead, you are someone who has internalized the fear of being these things and who has since experienced tremendous discomfort because of it.

Transforming Your Identity

Transforming your identity requires you to discover how you are identifying yourself now and how you ought to identify yourself for you to become who you are. You mustn't kneecap your reports in this process. In other words, don't minimize them or choose weak descriptions for yourself. Instead, pick ones that affirm who you are with certainty, strength, and power.

For example: rather than Alicia saying, "I was recently promoted to partner at my firm, I'm still finding my place though," she needed to say, "I am a partner at a law firm." Instead of Ryan saying, "I have a wife and a newborn," he needed to say, "I am a husband and a father." Rather than saying, "I am studying finances to become an investment banker like my dad and grandpa," Chris needed to say, "I'm a university student." By owning who you are at an identity level with I am statements, you internalize who you really are and bring your thoughts up to speed with your current identity. Thus, you embrace your reality, and imposter syndrome has no reason to take root.

Chapter Summary

It is undeniable that your thoughts impact your reality. Transforming the way you describe yourself at an identity level is an excellent way of changing your reality and overcoming imposter syndrome by never giving it a chance to take root in the first place. You must describe your current identity with a present-tense, I-am statement, so your thoughts can catch up with your lived reality.

CHAPTER 15

Regulating Your Emotions to Overcome Imposter Syndrome

"What would life be if you had no courage to
attempt anything?" – Vincent Van Gogh

mbodying the reality of who you are at an identity level is an excellent way to facilitate transformation, but it only works if you are emotionally regulated. If you struggle with emotional dysregulation, no amount of attempting to shift your identity will work because you are too attached to the emotional outcomes of your imposter syndrome. You must learn emotional self-regulation to overcome imposter syndrome, then, as this will help you feel calmer and more balanced in situations that previously triggered you. With this balance, you can then appropriate your new identity and experience the breakthrough that comes with identity level change.

So, how do you emotionally regulate yourself?

Begin By Identifying Your Dysregulation

Many people do not recognize what dysregulation feels like because they're so used to it that they are unaware of it. Dysregulation occurs anytime we feel like something is unacceptable, unenjoyable, or otherwise "bad." How you feel when you experience imposter syndrome, for example, is a state of dysregulation. When you are regulated, you experience emotions like joy, contentment, and peace.

To begin identifying your dysregulation, it is easiest to take a notepad with you and jot down every time you notice a significant influx of unenjoyable emotions. Any time you are anxious, overwhelmed, angry, fearful, doubtful, uncertain, sad, irritated, frustrated, or otherwise discontent, you write it down. It helps also to write down what triggered the emotional state. As you get used to tracking this for 3-4 days, you will begin to see your emotions effortlessly. Soon, you will notice them sooner and sooner.

Start Cultivating Emotional Regulation

Noticing your dysregulated emotions is the first step of emotional regulation. The next step is to regulate them. Regulating your emotions is a skill many are not taught, which explains why many people experience things like imposter syndrome and cannot fathom a way to get beyond the emotions. Instead, they become trapped in them and begin to identify themselves as the emotional state they are experiencing.

Regulating your emotions is an entire book unto itself, but there are specific actions you can take to begin getting a handle on your emotional state. One way is to lean back into the mindfulness practice we discussed in chapter 9. By cultivating space for quiet and bringing awareness to how you feel and why you begin to acknowledge and validate your emotions. You can then practice letting them go. For truly troubling emotions, a more engaged practice like breathing, exercising, or even creating art may help you release the feelings and find a more profound sense of regulation.

Maintaining A Balanced Emotional State

If you only do steps one and two, you will do a fantastic job regulating your emotions, though you may still feel like you are on an emotional rollercoaster. The constant swing between dysregulated and regulated can feel overwhelming. An easier way to facilitate a breakthrough and experience ongoing relief from symptoms like imposter syndrome is to learn how to maintain a balanced emotional state.

Maintaining your balanced emotional state comes from developing intimacy with your emotions and regulating them immediately upon their arrival – or better yet when you anticipate them. Each emotion will likely have a unique way to manage it, for example journaling when you are sad or going for a run when you are angry. Learning these methods for yourself and using them to navigate emotions as they surface swiftly is a great way to maintain balance. You can also use them in advance if you anticipate a feeling will emerge based on the likely circumstances of your day.

For example, Kevin was a client I worked with that routinely experienced stress and imposter syndrome when he attended company meetings. In a boardroom full of various levels of executives and leaders at his company, he felt inferior. Rather than waiting for the feeling to surface, Kevin began regulating himself long before the meeting, immediately before it, and again after it with simple breathing practices. Because he was proactive due to his anticipation of the experience, Kevin began to experience relief in these scenarios and felt more confident and courageous in board meetings.

Chapter Summary

Emotional dysregulation is a common state that people experience. It occurs when we do not know how to manage our emotions. A great way to create emotional regulation in your life is to identify dysregulation. Then, you can start learning how to regulate your emotions. As you become more comfortable with emotional regulation, you can do it proactively and maintain a balanced emotional state rather than riding the rollercoaster of dysregulation and regulation.

CHAPTER 16

Building Your Self-Control
and Self-Discipline

"You can never conquer the mountain.
You can only conquer yourself."
— Jim Whittaker

M any people are entirely unaware of how powerful they indeed are. Especially when they are struggling with feelings of anxiety, self-doubt, and inadequacy, it can be challenging to recall how capable you are. Because of this mindset, maintaining self-control and self-discipline can feel impossible. Essentially, you become emotionally hijacked and "forget" about your strengths. This is where the emotional regulation we discussed in the last chapter comes in handy.

There is an additional step you can take, however, to get even more robust results. That is self-control and self-discipline.

Why Don't We Have Self-Control?

A lack of self-control generally comes from a failure to recognize that you are the ultimate ruler of your mind. You might experience emotional hijackings that bring about your own troubling thoughts, but this doesn't mean you *are* your emotions or your thoughts. It means you experience them and have yet to learn to control them.

Quite simply, self-control comes from giving yourself an order and following through. Self-discipline comes from holding yourself accountable to giving and completing orders you give yourself.

This seems unacceptable to people who lack self-control, but it is a reality that if you train yourself to follow your own rules, you can control your mind. Let's explore how.

How To Become Self-Disciplined

If you were to give yourself a command and follow through on it, we would call that self-control. For example, if you commanded yourself to tie your shoelaces and do so, you have completed an act of self-control. Many people can do this with simple tasks, but with more challenging tasks, they feel defeated. This isn't because they *can't* have self-control in those more difficult areas. It's actually because they don't have the *experience*.

Building self-control and self-discipline take time. It requires you to focus your effort on commands and follow through and do so enough times that you begin to build trust and confidence in yourself. As you do, you can increase the complexity of the commands and, therefore, your trust and confidence in yourself.

With imposter syndrome, an excellent way is to reflect on Kevin from the previous chapter. I noted how Kevin transformed his emotional regulation skills around his boardroom meetings with breathing. What you might not have picked up on, however, was that for this to have a positive outcome, Kevin needed to *act on it*. This means he needed to give himself the command to breathe and then *do it*.

As you gain control over your imposter syndrome, you will need to do the same. In other words: you will need to not only read the skills you've learned about in this book but practice giving yourself the command to act on them and then do it. If you make a mistake or don't get the exact outcome you desire, you must keep giving yourself commands and acting on them to the best of your ability until you get the result you desire.

Chapter Summary

Self-control is the ability to give yourself a command and follow it. Self-discipline is holding yourself accountable to regularly give yourself orders and follow through on them. Many people lack this ability because they are not aware that they can give themselves a set of rules and expect themselves to follow them.

By building your self-control and self-discipline, however, you can experience significant relief from imposter syndrome and other troubling feelings because you have deliberately taken back your power from overwhelming thoughts and emotions. You can then eliminate the symptoms you experience due to imposter syndrome by deliberately choosing different coping mechanisms that bring more substantial relief. If self-control is not something you currently possess you can build it with regular daily action steps. It is advised to start with easy commands and build your way up to following through on more challenging ones. This way, you trust yourself when it is time to execute your self-discipline and change your experience with imposter syndrome.

CHAPTER 17

Becoming Your Most Compassionate Supporter

"Believe in your infinite potential. Your only
limitations are those you set upon yourself."
– Roy T. Bennett

The degree to which you believe in yourself and the standard to which you hold yourself become the level you rise to in life. Many people do not believe in themselves or hold themselves to unhelpful standards because this is what they have been taught to do. Their parents taught them they were the less intelligent sibling, their peers taught them they were the less attractive mate, and their teachers taught them they were the less agreeable pupil. Everyone has a story about the people who thought less of them and how they did so.

Unfortunately, most people are letting these false narratives drive their entire life. Taking back your power, then, includes seeing your dreams as worthy enough, yourself as good enough, and your results as successful enough. By validating yourself to have all the 'enough' you need, you release your need to meet anyone else's expectations and instead focus on meeting your own.

This is what Chris from much earlier in this book had to do. While his father and grandfather were abundantly supportive of him, he still felt inadequate. Why? Because people had compared him to his father and grandfather for as long as he could remember. His mathematical skills, charisma, charm, friendliness, networking abilities, business sense, intelligence, and even his looks were constantly commented on by others. They wanted to know if he would be as intelligent as his father and grandfather, as capable of running the business, and as attractive in such a position. None of them cared about how he felt about what he was hearing. They were simply passing ignorant remarks.

Regardless of how often Chris's father and grandfather praised him, he felt inadequate. It was only when he became his most prominent supporter that he began to feel a strong sense of confidence and competence in himself.

Discarding Other's Limitations

Discarding other people's limits is often as simple as having a genuine heart-to-heart with yourself. Begin by identifying what limitations you have bought into, who they came from, and why you cared enough to accept them as your own. For example, was your dad critical of your professional aspirations? Perhaps you bought his critique because you valued his opinion and wanted to please him.

The next step is to recognize that their limitations are not serving you and decide what belief *would* benefit you. For example, refraining from following your passions because they do not please your dad is not logical, nor is it supportive of living a good life. Instead, you can focus on the truth that your satisfaction is your responsibility, and your fulfillment is more important than your dad's approval. You can also recognize that there are other ways to experience joyous moments with your dad that do not include you choosing your entire lifestyle around his desires for you.

Based on this example, you can see how a simple breakdown of how beliefs can be acknowledged and remedied in a matter of moments. From there, you must employ self-confidence and self-discipline to stay on the path of following *your* belief rather than someone else's limitation.

Cheering Yourself On (Through Anything)

After you have done the job of discarding limiting beliefs, you can begin to do the work of cheering yourself on! This step is essential for two reasons: it builds your confidence and self-esteem, and it helps build momentum around your new belief. If you are genuinely pleased with yourself and satisfied with your results, the belief that you are capable, worthy, and successful becomes easier to believe.

Cheering yourself on can include using positive affirmations, taking yourself out for a celebratory dinner, speaking highly of yourself in the presence of others and yourself, and updating your identity to match the truth of what you are capable of. You might celebrate yourself with a trip somewhere, a nice outfit, a bath, a delicious meal, or with anything else that makes you feel celebrated and successful.

The more you celebrate yourself and become your biggest supporter, the stronger your joy and confidence will become, and the less you will experience imposter syndrome.

Cheering Even When It Seems "Small"

A final point I want to make is that it is important to cheer yourself on even for seemingly "small" things. When you struggle with imposter syndrome it is easy to minimize your efforts and successes. You might feel that you must reach new achievements continually to be considered worthy of praise. Unfortunately, it is all too easy to set that standard higher each time you reach a new goal.

Make a point to celebrate yourself even when it seems small. Celebrate days when you did your best, when things didn't go as planned but you learned something along the way, and when you discover something that will help you achieve your desired outcome later. Consider any and all progress worthy of celebration. Even if that celebration is as simple as acknowledging yourself for a job well done, it matters. In addition to helping you feel good about your progress this will build your self-esteem and self-confidence allowing you to grow beyond imposter syndrome.

Chapter Summary

If you are still trapped in the limiting beliefs of others, chances are you struggle to celebrate yourself because you don't see yourself as worthy or capable. You can choose to change this, however, by discarding the limiting beliefs of others, believing in yourself, and actively cheering yourself on through life. The more you lean into being your own biggest supporter, the less imposter syndrome will be able to latch on and hold you back from your dreams. There are many ways to cheer yourself on. Each of us has different actions that make us feel celebrated. It is worth it to discover what actions make you feel celebrated so you can celebrate yourself in ways that feel good.

CHAPTER 18

Embracing Your Innate Strengths

"Once you embrace your value, talents, and strength,
it neutralizes when others think less of you."
– Rob Liano

Your strengths are equally as crucial as your weaknesses, and you have much more to offer you. While your shortcomings keep you humble and help you make plans to overcome things you may have difficulty with, your strengths propel you forward. Too many people suffering from imposter syndrome ignore their strengths and spend a lengthy amount of time apologizing for their weaknesses. This backward approach holds you back from having a desirable outcome in life because you never benefit from the many things you are capable of. In the absolute worst-case scenario, you believe you are incapable of *anything* and hold yourself back entirely.

Regardless of where you land on this spectrum, it is inevitable and unquestionable that you have unique strengths that you bring to the table in all areas of life. Whether it's your career or studies like Alicia and Chris, in your relationship like Ryan, at the gym like Eric, or anywhere else in your life. You have innate talents and abilities that you can lean into and expand on if you wish to.

When dealing with something as troubling as imposter syndrome, I believe you *must*.

Identifying Your Personal Strengths

There are three excellent ways to identify your strengths. The first one is simple: ask others. What do your family, friends, and colleagues believe you are good at? What do they see you excelling with? The people in our lives tend to have kinder feedback for us than we do for ourselves, and they see us from an outside perspective. This means they do not have all the self-depreciating thoughts going on about you that you might have. Thus, their feedback is likely to be more accurate.

Another way you can identify your strengths is to reflect on things you like to do that you generally get great results with. Knowing the strengths that align with your interests is a great way to identify strengths you can expand on that also bring you satisfaction and joy in life. Often, doing what brings you joy is a great way to grow beyond imposter syndrome because you genuinely have fun with the learning and growing process. Therefore, imposter syndrome is less likely to take root.

Finally, you can look at your accomplishments. What awards or praise have you received in your life, and why? What skills brought you to those successes? It is fair to say that if you have enough skills to generate desirable results in these areas of your life, you have tapped into a strength.

Having Faith In Your Ability

An essential part of identifying your strengths is having faith in them and your ability to repeatedly succeed with them. Imposter syndrome often brings about the feeling that you have won *by luck.* Remember Ryan in part two? He believed luck landed him his wife and not his personality and likability. The trouble with this type of belief is that you weaken your power by giving away credit for how you created your results. In doing so, you turn your genuine strength into a random act of circumstance.

You can have faith in and take responsibility for your strengths by taking a moment to identify all the ways those strengths have helped you. In what ways did those strengths help you achieve the many successes you have achieved?

For example, if you have strong people skills and need to build credibility in this skill with yourself, you might acknowledge how these skills have helped you build beautiful friendships, earn an incredible partner, advance through your career, enjoy positive peer experiences in school, and anything else they have helped you with.

Building the case, so to speak, for these skills helps you recognize that they are genuine strengths that you have benefitted from many times. Naturally, you do not realize this because they come so easy to you, yet they are still strengths!

Chapter Summary

Imposter syndrome has an uncanny ability to convince us that we only have weaknesses and that our strengths are unimportant or random. Of course, this is not at all the case. Learning to recognize your strengths and building your faith in them allows you to see that you bring many beautiful talents to the table in all areas of your life. Realize that strengths come in all shapes and sizes and that all your strengths are equally important to your success. Taking the time to recognize and celebrate this is essential.

Further, if you combine this with cheering yourself on and emotional regulation, you can create a breakthrough that allows you to recognize how powerful and capable you are. Together, they help you build yourself up and see yourself in a more balanced light.

CHAPTER 19

Healing Perfectionism And Stopping Imposter Syndrome In Its Tracks

"Perfectionism rarely begets perfection, or
satisfaction – only disappointment."
– Ryan Holiday

Peoople who experience imposter syndrome also tend to experience perfectionism. Perfectionism can fuel imposter syndrome by causing you to set unrealistic standards for yourself and feel like an imposter any time you do not reach them. You may also falsely believe that other people are routinely getting these results, making you feel worse.

Healing imposter syndrome and healing perfectionism, then, are often one and the same. In this chapter, we will dive into a final breakthrough with steps on overcoming perfectionism so you can set realistic standards and feel good about your ability to achieve them.

Become Aware Of Your Perfectionism

Self-awareness is always the first step of change. When healing from perfectionism-induced imposter syndrome, becoming aware of your perfectionism is a great way to understand where these symptoms are leaking in, how, and why.

The easiest way to become aware of your perfectionism is to ask yourself these questions:

1. What unrealistic standards are you setting for yourself?
2. What are these unrealistic standards trying to protect you from?
3. Why are you afraid of setting more realistic standards?
4. What are you giving up every time your perfectionism pushes you to work harder, do more, or prove yourself?

Understanding your answers to these questions helps you see where perfectionism is holding you back, how, and why. You can then begin to heal perfectionism and relieve yourself of the subsequent imposter syndrome it causes.

Break Your Tasks Into Easier Sizes

Perfectionism can easily take root when we focus on dream-sized goals. Because they are so large and far away, it is easy to make them lofty with dazzling desires that seem unachievable from where you are. The trouble with this approach is that you inevitably make it so large that you cannot conceive how to take action right now. This takes your perfectionism to the next level by keeping you stuck in inaction because you cannot possibly achieve those outcomes from where you are.

Breaking your dreams and big tasks into bite-sized pieces helps you set your sights on a more manageable and realistic goal. As you achieve those goals, you *feel* like you are accomplishing something. This builds momentum and brings you closer to your big dreams while eliminating perfectionism and imposter syndrome. That's because, rather than trying to live from the results, you are living from where you are now and creating those results each day increasingly.

Give Your Standards A Reality Check

Reality checks can be uncomfortable, but they are also humbling and helpful. Occasionally, you need to give yourself a reality check to ensure that the standards you hold to are realistic and practical rather than unrealistic and harmful.

You can give yourself a reality check by looking at your goals from two perspectives. First, look at your "big goal." This is the outcome you are aiming for. Check in with yourself by asking yourself: is this something I want and am willing to work toward? Do I believe I am capable of creating this outcome? A high-quality goal is something you may not know how to achieve, and it may feel "out there," but it motivates you to grow. Your "big goals" *should* be a little unrealistic.

Now, I want you to look at your "next step" toward the big goal. What is it? Is it realistic based on where you are right now? Do you have the skills and ability to reach this next step? If you don't, do you have the necessary resources to gain the skills or knowledge? Your next step should always be a lot more sensible and achievable. These are the accessible steps that build up to the lofty outcome. An excellent marker to determine if you are working toward realistic next steps is to consider whether you can take action on that next step *today.* If you can't, it may be unrealistic.

Finally, reflect on what you think about yourself. Are you compassionate to yourself? Do you have grace with yourself during the learning process? Are you okay with making mistakes and learning from them? Are you being kind to yourself? If you answer "no" to any of these questions, you may need to be more realistic with yourself.

Chapter Summary

Perfectionism often accompanies imposter syndrome and makes the symptoms even worse. This is because perfectionism causes you to have unrealistic standards and feel guilty or ashamed when you can't reach them. Sometimes, your standards might even cause you to self-sabotage because they create fear or anxiety around taking action or maintaining progress with your goals. Every case study I presented you in this book was of a person whose imposter syndrome was being enhanced by perfectionism. Identifying symptoms of perfectionism is essential to helping you understand how this mindset worsens imposter syndrome. You can then focus on creating bite-sized goals and giving yourself a reality check about the standards you're holding yourself to with your goals, next steps, and day-to-day actions.

CONCLUSION

"No one can make you feel inferior without your consent." – Eleanor Roosevelt

Imposter syndrome is a troubling mindset that can significantly hold you back. Left unchecked, it can prevent you from ever acting on your biggest dreams or pursuing your desired life. For some people, it can become so self-sabotaging that not only does it hold them back from what they want, it can move them in the opposite direction of their dreams.

In this book, *Imposter Syndrome Anecdotes: Techniques For Overcoming Imposter Syndrome And Live The Life Of Your Dreams*, we have discussed the necessary action you can take to overcome imposter syndrome once and for all. This doesn't mean it will be easy, nor that will your relief come overnight. It *will* take significant effort to continually employ the practices we have discussed in this book to ensure you experience relief from your symptoms.

While imposter syndrome is not an official diagnosis, it still has a significant impact on people's lives and requires them to take serious action to remedy it. The more seriously you take this process, the better your results will be.

After reading this book cover to cover, I strongly encourage you to keep it handy and continue to reread it. For your second reading, you can focus on the areas you need help with most. These are likely the areas that, upon your first reading, you felt *most* impacted by the words you read. By focusing on these areas, you build momentum toward relieving yourself of the self-doubt, anxiety, and unworthiness that imposter syndrome brings.

It is essential that you don't just read this book but that you also take the time to implement the actions you learn. The stronger your self-control and self-discipline are, the more you will gain from this book. Remember, too, that these are skills you can build on. So, if you are not presently experiencing the complete relief of them, you can begin building on them by giving yourself commands and following through and by holding yourself accountable for your efforts.

Over time, your momentum will build. Then, seemingly all at once, you will see everything transform before your eyes. "Suddenly," imposter syndrome will not be such a concern for you. It will be a thing of the past as you find yourself continually growing positively with the momentum you have created.

With that being said, I ask that before you dig back into the pages of this book, you take a moment to please review *Imposter Syndrome Anecdotes: Techniques For Overcoming Imposter Syndrome And Live The Life Of Your Dreams* on Amazon Kindle! Your honest feedback would be greatly appreciated.

Thank you, and best of luck in overcoming your imposter syndrome!

SALES DESCRIPTION

Discover specific, actionable methods you can use to overcome imposter syndrome once and for all. It's time to stop limiting yourself with self-doubt and feelings of unworthiness and start living the life you are capable of.

While it is not an official mental health diagnosis, imposter syndrome is a widely recognized phenomenon that negatively impacts mental health. Those suffering generally feel low self-worth, and high self-doubt and engage in several self-sabotaging behaviors that hold them back from living a life that brings them fulfillment and joy.

Changing your experience with imposter syndrome begins by understanding what this condition is and how it impacts you. In Part 1 of *Imposter Syndrome Anecdotes: Techniques For Overcoming Imposter Syndrome And Live The Life Of Your Dreams*, that is precisely what we dig into. From there, we move into steps you can take to overcome imposter syndrome and the unique ways it impacts your life.

We do this in a three-step process.

First, we will uncover steps you can take to gain immediate relief from imposter syndrome and expand that relief over time. The more you implement these practices, the more the momentum will build, and the stronger your relief. For that reason, it is advised that you make them a part of your regular routine.

This includes things like:

- Daily affirmations
- Building your positive mindset
- Adopting a growth mindset
- Practicing visualization
- Engaging in positive self-talk
- Employing mindfulness
- Building positive coping mechanisms

In the second step, we focus on body language and how it impacts imposter syndrome. Here, we dig into a system called 'biofeedback,' which has a significant impact on the way you feel about yourself. Biofeedback, as you will learn, is the process of your thoughts being impacted by your physical reality. Body language is a tangible practice to positively influence your psyche with your physical actions.

We will discuss two levels of body language:

- How you carry yourself; and,
- How you interact with others

161

Finally, we will lean into imposter syndrome breakthroughs. These are generally not considered to be repeatable or sustainable long-term. Still, they can provide enough of a breakthrough in your imposter syndrome thought cycle to change your experience. These breakthroughs are facilitated with reality checks, self-awareness, and practices that help you transform how you see yourself and your circumstances.

They include things like:

- Changing your narrative
- Regulating your emotions
- Building self-confidence and self-discipline
- Becoming your own cheerleader
- Embracing your strengths
- Healing perfectionism

By following this three-step process, you will eliminate imposter syndrome for good. Let me be clear: it will take effort and consistency, but the results will be worth the effort. Purchase your copy of *Imposter Syndrome Anecdotes: Techniques For Overcoming Imposter Syndrome And Live The Life Of Your Dreams* to discover the relief this book can provide!

Made in United States
Orlando, FL
13 September 2023

36934669R00095